YOUR]
HOROSCOPE
2008

AQUARIUS

YOUR PERSONAL
HOROSCOPE
2008

AQUARIUS
21st January–19th February

igloo

igloo

This edition published by Igloo Books Ltd,
Cottage Farm, Mears Ashby Road, Sywell, Northants NN6 0BJ
www.igloo-books.com
E-mail: Info@igloo-books.com

Produced for Igloo Books by W. Foulsham & Co. Ltd,
The Publishing House, Bennetts Close, Cippenham,
Slough, Berkshire SL1 5AP, England

ISBN: 978-1-845-61617-5

This is an abridged version of material
originally published in *Old Moore's Horoscope
and Astral Diary*.

Printed in China

CONTENTS

INTRODUCTION

Your Personal Horoscopes have been specifically created to allow you to get the most from astrological patterns and the way they have a bearing on not only your zodiac sign, but nuances within it. Using the diary section of the book you can read about the influences and possibilities of each and every day of the year. It will be possible for you to see when you are likely to be cheerful and happy or those times when your nature is in retreat and you will be more circumspect. The diary will help to give you a feel for the specific 'cycles' of astrology and the way they can subtly change your day-to-day life. For example, when you see the sign ☿, this means that the planet Mercury is retrograde at that time. Retrograde means it appears to be running backwards through the zodiac. Such a happening has a significant effect on communication skills, but this is only one small aspect of how the Personal Horoscope can help you.

With Your Personal Horoscope the story doesn't end with the diary pages. It includes simple ways for you to work out the zodiac sign the Moon occupied at the time of your birth, and what this means for your personality. In addition, if you know the time of day you were born, it is possible to discover your Ascendant, yet another important guide to your personal make-up and potential.

Many readers are interested in relationships and in knowing how well they get on with people of other astrological signs. You might also be interested in the way you appear to very different sorts of individuals. If you are such a person, the section on Venus will be of particular interest. Despite the rapidly changing position of this planet, you can work out your Venus sign, and learn what bearing it will have on your life.

Using Your Personal Horoscope you can travel on one of the most fascinating and rewarding journeys that anyone can take – the journey to a better realisation of self.

THE ESSENCE OF AQUARIUS

Exploring the Personality of Aquarius the Water Carrier

(21ST JANUARY– 19TH FEBRUARY)

What's in a sign?

Oh, what a wonderful person you can be! Despite a number of contradictions and one of the most complicated natures to be found anywhere in the zodiac, you certainly know how to make friends and influence people. Your ruling planet is Uranus, one of the more recently discovered members of the solar system's family. It rules modern communications, such as radio and television, and also has a response to the recent discoveries of science. It is within the world of 'the modern' that you reside and you have little or no difficulty keeping up with the ever-increasing pace of life.

People naturally like you and it's not surprising. You are open, liberal, and rarely judgmental, and you are often surrounded by deeply original and even eccentric types. Life to you is a storybook full of fascinating tales. Aquarians amass information 'on the hoof' and very little passes you by. Understanding what makes others tick is meat and drink to you and proves to be a source of endless joy. Unlike the other Air signs of Gemini and Libra, you are able to spend long hours on your own if necessary and always keep your mind active.

Aquarians have great creative potential; they are refined, often extremely well educated and they remain totally classless. This makes it easy for you to get on with just about any sort of person and also explains your general success in the material world. You are fascinating, original, thought-provoking and even quite deep on occasions. Matters that take months for others to synthesise, you can absorb in minutes. It is clear to everyone that you are one of life's natural leaders, but when you head any organisation you do so by co-operation and example because you are not in the least authoritarian.

In love you can be ardent and sincere – for a while at least. You need to be loved and it's true that deeply personal relationships can be a problem to you if they are not supplying what is most important to you. Few people know the real you, because your nature exists on so many different levels. For this reason alone you defy analysis and tend to remain outside the scope of orthodoxy. And because people can't weigh you up adequately, you appear to be more fascinating than ever.

Aquarius resources

Your chief resource has to be originality. Like a precious Fabergé Egg you are a single creation, unique and quite unlike anything else to be found anywhere in the world. Of course, used wrongly, this can make you seem odd or even downright peculiar. But Aquarians usually have a knack for creating the best possible impression. The chances are that you dress in your own way and speak the words that occur to you, and that you have a side to your nature that shuns convention. Despite this you know how to adapt when necessary. As a result your dinner parties would sport guests of a wide variety of types and stations. All of these people think they know the 'real you' and remain committed to helping you as much as they can.

The natural adaptability that goes along with being an Aquarian makes it possible for you to turn your hand to many different projects. And because you are from an Air sign, you can undertake a variety of tasks at the same time. This makes for a busy life, but being on the go is vital for you and you only tire when you are forced into jobs that you find demeaning, pointless or downright dull.

All of the above combines to make a nature that has 'resourcefulness' as its middle name. Arriving at a given set of circumstances – say a specific task that has to be undertaken – you first analyse what is required. Having done so you get cracking and invariably manage to impress all manner of people with your dexterity, attention to detail and downright intelligence. You can turn work into a social event, or derive financial gain from your social life. Activity is the keyword and you don't really differentiate between the various components of life as many people would.

Success depends on a number of different factors. You need to be doing things you enjoy as much you can and you simply cannot be held back or bound to follow rules that appear to make no sense to you. You respond well to kindness, and generally receive it because you are so considerate yourself. But perhaps your greatest skill of all is your ability to make a silk purse out of a sow's ear. You are never stuck for an idea and rarely let financial restrictions get in your way.

Beneath the surface

'What you see is what you get' could never really be considered a sensible or accurate statement when applied to the sign of Aquarius. It's difficult enough for you to know the way your complicated mind works, and almost impossible for others to sort out the tangle of possibilities. Your mind can be as untidy as a tatty workbox on occasions and yet at other times you can see through situations with a clarity that would dazzle almost any observer. It really depends on a whole host of circumstances, some of which are inevitably beyond your own control. You are at your best when you are allowed to take charge from the very start of any project, because then your originality of thought comes into play. Your sort of logic is unique to you, so don't expect anyone else to go down the same mental routes that you find easy to follow.

Aquarians are naturally kind and don't tend to discriminate. This is not a considered matter, it's simply the way you are. As a result it is very hard for you to understand prejudice, or individuals who show any form of intolerance. The fairness that you exemplify isn't something that you have to work at – it comes as naturally to you as breathing does.

You can be very peculiar and even a little cranky on occasions. These aspects of your nature are unlikely to have any bearing on your overall popularity, but they do betray a rather unusual mindset that isn't like that of any other zodiac sign. When you feel stressed you tend to withdraw into yourself, which is not really good for you. A much better strategy would be to verbalise what you are thinking, even though this is not always particularly easy to do.

There are many people in the world who think they know you well, but each and every one of them knows only one Aquarian. There are always more, each a unique individual and probably as much of a mystery to you as they would be to all your relatives and friends, that is if any of them suspected just how deep and mysterious you can be. Despite these facts, your mind is clear and concise, enabling you to get to the truth of any given situation almost immediately. You should never doubt your intuitive foresight and, in the main, must always back your hunches. It is rare indeed for you to be totally wrong about the outcome of any potential situation and your genuine originality of thought is the greatest gift providence has bestowed on you.

Making the best of yourself

Interacting with the world is most important to you. Although you can sometimes be a good deal quieter than the other Air signs of Gemini and Libra, you are still a born communicator, with a great need to live your life to the full. If you feel hemmed in or constrained by circumstances, you are not going to show your best face to family, friends or colleagues. That's why you must move heaven and earth to make certain that you are not tied down in any way. Maintaining a sense of freedom is really just a mental state to Aquarius but it is absolutely vital to your well-being.

As far as work is concerned you need to be doing something that allows you the room you need to move. Any occupation that means thinking on your feet would probably suit you fine. All the same you feel more comfortable in administrative surroundings, rather than getting your hands dirty. Any profession that brings change and variety on a daily basis would be best. You are a good team operator, and yet can easily lead from the front. Don't be frightened to show colleagues that you have an original way of looking at life and that you are an inveterate problem solver.

In terms of friendship you tend to be quite catholic in your choice of pals. Making the best of yourself means keeping things that way. You are not naturally jealous yourself but you do tend to attract friends who are. Make it plain that you can't tie yourself down to any one association, no matter how old or close it may be. At least if you do this nobody can suggest that they weren't warned when you wander off to talk to someone else. Personal relationships are a different matter, though it's hardly likely that you would live in the pocket of your partner. In any situation you need space to breathe, and this includes romantic attachments. People who know you well will not try to hem you in.

Don't be frightened to show your unconventional, even wild side to the world at large. You are a bold character, with a great deal to say and a natural warmth that could melt an iceberg. This is the way providence made you and it is only right to use your gifts to the full.

The impressions you give

You are not a naturally secretive person and don't hold back very much when it comes to speaking your mind. It might be suggested therefore that the external and internal Aquarian is more or less the same person. Although generally true, it has to be remembered that you have a multi-faceted nature and one that adapts quickly to changing circumstances. It is this very adaptability that sets you apart in the eyes of the world.

You often make decisions based on intuitive foresight and although many Aquarians are of above average intelligence, you won't always make use of a deep knowledge of any given situation. In essence you often do what seems right, though you tend to act whilst others are still standing around and thinking. This makes you good to have around in a crisis and convinces many of those looking on that you are incredibly capable, relaxed and confident. Of course this isn't always the case, but even a nervous interior tends to breed outward action in the case of your zodiac sign, so the world can be forgiven for jumping to the wrong conclusion.

People like you – there's no doubt about that. However, you must realise that you have a very upfront attitude, which on occasions is going to get you into trouble. Your occasional weirdness, rather than being a turn-off, is likely to stimulate the interest that the world has in you. Those with whom you come into contract invariably find your personality to be attractive, generous, high-spirited and refreshing. For all these reasons it is very unlikely that you would actually make many enemies, even if some folk are clearly jealous of the easy way you have with the world.

One of the great things about Aquarians is that they love to join in. As a result you may find yourself doing all sorts of things that others would find either difficult or frightening. You can be zany, wild and even mad on occasions, but these tendencies will only get you liked all the more. The world will only tire of you if you allow yourself to get down in the dumps or grumpy – a very rare state for Aquarius.

The way forward

In terms of living your life to the full it is probable that you don't need any real advice from an astrologer. Your confidence allows you to go places that would make some people shiver, whilst your intuitive foresight gives you the armoury you need to deal with a world that can sometimes seem threatening. Yet for all this you are not immune to mental turmoil on occasions, and probably spend rather too much time in the fast lane. It's good to rest, a fact that you need to remember the next time you find yourself surrounded by twenty-seven jobs, all of which you are trying to undertake at the same time.

The more the world turns in the direction of information technology, the happier you are likely to become. If others have difficulty in this age of computers, it's likely that you relish the challenges and the opportunities that these artificial intelligences offer. You are happy with New Age concepts and tend to look at the world with compassion and understanding. Despite the fact that you are always on the go, it's rare for you to be moving forward so fast that you forget either the planet that brought you to birth, or the many underprivileged people who inhabit parts of it. You have a highly developed conscience and tend to work for the good of humanity whenever you can.

You might not be constructed of the highest moral fibre known to humanity, a fact that sometimes shows when it comes to romantic attachments. Many Aquarians play the field at some time in their lives and it's certain that you need a personal relationship that keeps you mentally stimulated. Although your exterior can sometimes seem superficial, you have a deep and sensitive soul – so perhaps you should marry a poet, or at least someone who can cope with the twists and turns of the Aquarian mind. Aquarians who tie themselves down too early, or to the wrong sort of individual, invariable end up regretting the fact.

You can be deeply creative and need to live in clean and cheerful surroundings. Though not exactly a minimalist you don't like clutter and constantly need to spring-clean your home – and your mind. Living with others isn't difficult for you, in fact it's essential. Since you are so adaptable you fit in easily into almost any environment, though you will always ultimately stamp your own character onto it. You love to be loved and offer a great deal in return, even if you are occasionally absent when people need you the most. In essence you are in love with life and so perhaps you should not be too surprised to discover that it is very fond of you too.

14

AQUARIUS ON THE CUSP

Astrological profiles are altered for those people born at either the beginning or the end of a zodiac sign, or, more properly, on the cusps of a sign. In the case of Aquarius this would be on the 21st of January and for two or three days after, and similarly at the end of the sign, probably from the 17th to the 19th of February.

The Capricorn Cusp – January 21st to 23rd

What really sets you apart is a genuinely practical streak that isn't always present in the sign of Aquarius when taken alone. You are likely to have all the joy of life and much of the devil-may-care attitude of your Sun sign, but at the same time you are capable of getting things done in a very positive way. This makes you likely to achieve a higher degree of material success and means that you ally managerial skills with the potential for rolling up your sleeves and taking part in the 'real work' yourself. Alongside this you are able to harness the naturally intuitive qualities of Aquarius in a very matter-of-fact way. Few people would have the ability to pull the wool over your eyes and you are rarely stuck for a solution, even to apparently difficult problems.

You express yourself less well than Aquarius taken alone, and you may have a sort of reserve that leads others to believe that your mind is full of still waters which run very deep. The air of mystery can actually be quite useful, because it masks an ability to react and move quickly when necessary, which is a great surprise to the people around you. However, there are two sides to every coin and if there is a slightly negative quality to this cuspid position it might lie in the fact that you are not quite the communicator that tends to be the case with Aquarius, and you could go through some fairly quiet and introspective phases that those around you would find somewhat difficult to understand. In a positive sense this offers a fairly wistful aspect to your nature that may, in romantic applications, appear very attractive. There is something deeply magnetic about your nature and it isn't quite possible for everyone to understand what makes you tick. Actually this is part of your appeal because there is nothing like curiosity on the part of others to enhance your profile.

Getting things done is what matters the most to you, harnessed to the ability to see the wider picture in life. It's true that not everyone understands your complex nature, but in friendship you are scarcely short of supportive types. Family members can be especially important to you and personal attachments are invariably made for life.

The Pisces Cusp – February 17th to 19th

It appears that you are more of a thinker than most and achieve depths of contemplation that would be totally alien to some signs of the zodiac. Much of your life is given over to the service you show for humanity as a whole but you don't sink into the depths of despair in the way that some Piscean individuals are inclined to do. You are immensely likeable and rarely stuck for a good idea. You know how to enjoy yourself, even if this quality is usually tied to the support and assistance that you constantly give to those around you.

Many of you will already have chosen a profession that somehow fulfils your need to be of service, and it isn't unusual for Pisces-cusp Aquarians to alter their path in life totally if it isn't fulfilling this most basic requirement. When necessary, you can turn your hand to almost anything, generally giving yourself totally to the task in hand, sometimes to the exclusion of everything else. People with this combination often have two very different sorts of career, sometimes managing to do both at the same time. Confidence in practical matters isn't usually lacking, even if you sometimes think that your thought processes are a little bit muddled.

In love you are ardent and more sincere than Aquarius sometimes seems to be. There can be a tinge of jealousy at work now and again in deep relationships, but you are less likely than Pisces to let this show. You tend to be very protective of the people who are most important in your life and these are probably fewer in number than often seems to be the case for Aquarius. Your love of humanity and the needs it has of you are of supreme importance and you barely let a day pass without offering some sort of assistance. For this reason, and many others, you are a much loved individual and show your most caring face to the world for the majority of your life. Material success can be hard to come by at first, but it isn't really an aspect of life that worries you too much in any case. It is far more important for you to be content with your lot and, if you are happy, it seems that more or less everything else tends to follow.

AQUARIUS AND ITS ASCENDANTS

The nature of every individual on the planet is composed of the rich variety of zodiac signs and planetary positions that were present at the time of their birth. Your Sun sign, which in your case is Aquarius, is one of the many factors when it comes to assessing the unique person you are. Probably the most important consideration, other than your Sun sign, is to establish the zodiac sign that was rising over the eastern horizon at the time that you were born. This is your Ascending or Rising sign. Most popular astrology fails to take account of the Ascendant, and yet its importance remains with you from the very moment of your birth, through every day of your life. The Ascendant is evident in the way you approach the world, and so, when meeting a person for the first time, it is this astrological influence that you are most likely to notice first. Our Ascending sign essentially represents what we appear to be, while the Sun sign is what we feel inside ourselves.

The Ascendant also has the potential for modifying our overall nature. For example, if you were born at a time of day when Aquarius was passing over the eastern horizon (this would be around the time of dawn) then you would be classed as a double Aquarian. As such, you would typify this zodiac sign, both internally and in your dealings with others. However, if your Ascendant sign turned out to be a Fire sign, such as Aries, there would be a profound alteration of nature, away from the expected qualities of Aquarius.

One of the reasons why popular astrology often ignores the Ascendant is that it has always been rather difficult to establish. We have found a way to make this possible by devising an easy-to-use table, which you will find on page 157 of this book. Using this, you can establish your Ascendant sign at a glance. You will need to know your rough time of birth, then it is simply a case of following the instructions.

For those readers who have no idea of their time of birth it might be worth allowing a good friend, or perhaps your partner, to read through the section that follows this introduction. Someone who deals with you on a regular basis may easily discover your Ascending sign, even though you could have some difficulty establishing it for yourself. A good understanding of this component of your nature is essential if you want to be aware of that 'other person' who is responsible for the way you make contact with the world at large. Your Sun sign, Ascendant sign, and the other pointers in this book will, together, allow you a far better understanding of what makes you tick as an individual. Peeling back the different layers of your astrological make-up can be an enlightening experience, and the Ascendant may represent one of the most important layers of all.

Aquarius with Aquarius Ascendant

You are totally unique and quite original, so much so that very few people could claim to understand what makes you tick. Routines get on your nerves and you need to be out there doing something most of the time. Getting where you want to go in life isn't too difficult, except that when you arrive, your destination might not look half so interesting as it did before. You are well liked and should have many friends. This is not to say that your pals have much in common with each other, because you choose from a wide cross-section of people. Although folks see you as being very reasonable in the main, you are capable of being quite cranky on occasions. Your intuition is extremely strong and is far less likely to let you down than would be the case with some individuals.

Travel is very important to you and you will probably live for some time in a different part of your own country, or even in another part of the world. At work you are more than capable, but do need something to do that you find personally stimulating, because you are not very good at constant routine. You can be relied upon to use your originality and find solutions that are instinctive and brilliant. Most people are very fond of you.

Aquarius with Pisces Ascendant

Here we find the originality of Aquarius balanced by the very sensitive qualities of Pisces, and it makes for a very interesting combination. When it comes to understanding other people you are second to none, but it's certain that you are more instinctive than either Pisces or Aquarius when taken alone. You are better at routines than Aquarius, but also relish a challenge more than the typical Piscean would. Active and enterprising, you tend to know what you want from life, but consideration of others, and the world at large, will always be part of the scenario. People with this combination often work on behalf of humanity and are to be found in social work, the medical profession and religious institutions. As far as beliefs are concerned you don't conform to established patterns, and yet may get closer to the truth of the Creator than many deep theological thinkers have ever been able to do. Acting on impulse as much as you do means that not everyone understands the way your mind works, but your popularity will invariably see you through.

Passionate and deeply sensitive, you are able to negotiate the twists and turns of a romantic life that is hardly likely to be run-of-the-mill. In the end, however, you should be able to discover a very deep personal and spiritual happiness.

Aquarius with Aries Ascendant

If ever anyone could be accused of setting off immediately, but slowly, it has to be you. These are very contradictory signs and the differences will express themselves in a variety of ways. One thing is certain, you have tremendous tenacity and will see a job through patiently from beginning to end, without tiring on the way and ensuring that every detail is taken care of properly. This combination often brings good health and a great capacity for continuity, particularly in terms of the length of life. You are certainly not as argumentative as the typical Aries, but you do know how to get your own way, which is just as well because you are usually thinking on behalf of everyone else and not just on your own account.

At home you can relax, which is a blessing for Aries, though in fact you seldom choose to do so because you always have some project or other on the go. You probably enjoy knocking down and rebuilding walls, though this is a practical tendency and not responsive to relationships, in which you are ardent and sincere. Impetuosity is as close to your heart as is the case for any type of subject, though you certainly have the ability to appear patient and steady. But it's just a front, isn't it?

Aquarius with Taurus Ascendant

There is nothing that you fail to think about deeply and with great intensity. You are wise, honest and very scientific in your approach to life. Routines are necessary in life but you have most of them sorted out well in advance and so always have time to look at the next interesting fact. If you don't spend all your time watching documentaries on the television set, you make a good friend and love to socialise. Most of the great discoveries of the world were probably made by people with this sort of astrological combination, though your nature is rather 'odd' on occasions and so can be rather difficult for others to understand.

You may be most surprised when others tell you that you are eccentric, but you don't really mind too much because for half of the time you are not inhabiting the same world as the rest of us. Because you can be delightfully dotty you are probably much loved and cherished by your friends, of which there are likely to be many. Family members probably adore you too, and you can be guaranteed to entertain anyone with whom you come into contact. The only fly in the ointment is that you sometimes lose track of reality, whatever that might be, and fly high in your own atmosphere of rarefied possibilities.

Aquarius with Gemini Ascendant

If you were around in the 1960s there is every chance that you were the first to go around with flowers in your hair. You are unconventional, original, quirky and entertaining. Few people would fail to notice your presence and you take life as it comes, even though on most occasions you are firmly in the driving seat. It all probability you care very much about the planet on which you live and the people with whom you share it. Not everyone understands you, but that does not really matter, for you have more than enough communication skills to put your message across intact. You should avoid wearing yourself out by worrying about things that you cannot control, and you definitely gain from taking time out to meditate. However, whether or not you allow yourself that luxury remains to be seen.

If you are not the most communicative form of Gemini subject then you must come a close second. Despite this fact much of what you have to say makes real sense and you revel in the company of interesting, intelligent and stimulating people, whose opinions on a host of matters will add to your own considerations. You are a true original in every sense of the word and the mere fact of your presence in the world is bound to add to the enjoyment of life experienced by the many people with whom you make contact.

Aquarius with Cancer Ascendant

The truly original spark, for which the sign of Aquarius is famed, can only enhance the caring qualities of Cancer, and is also inclined to bring the Crab out of its shell to a much greater extent than would be the case with certain other zodiac combinations. Aquarius is a party animal and never arrives without something interesting to say, which is doubly the case when the reservoir of emotion and consideration that is Cancer is feeding the tap. Your nature can be rather confusing for even you to deal with, but you are inspirational, bright, charming and definitely fun to be around.

The Cancer element in your nature means that you care about your home and the people to whom you are related. You are also a good and loyal friend, who would keep attachments for much longer than could be expected for Aquarius alone. You love to travel and can be expected to make many journeys to far-off places during your life. Some attention will have to be paid to your health, because you are capable of burning up masses of nervous energy, often without getting the periods of rest and contemplation that are essential to the deeper qualities of the sign of Cancer. Nevertheless you have determination, resilience and a refreshing attitude that lifts the spirits of the people in your vicinity.

Aquarius with Leo Ascendant

All associations with Aquarius bring originality, and you are no exception. You aspire to do your best most of the time but manage to achieve your objectives in an infinitely amusing and entertaining way. Not that you set out to do so, because if you are an actor on the stage of life, it seems as though you are a natural one. There is nothing remotely pretentious about your breezy personality or your ability to occupy the centre of any stage. This analogy is quite appropriate because you probably like the theatre. Being in any situation when reality is suspended for a while suits you down to the ground, and in any case you may regularly ask yourself if you even recognise what reality is. Always asking questions, both of yourself and the world at large, you soldier on relentlessly, though not to the exclusion of having a good time on the way.

Keeping to tried and tested paths is not your way. You are a natural trailblazer who is full of good ideas and who has the energy to put them into practice. You care deeply for the people who play an important part in your life but are wise enough to allow them the space they need to develop their own personalities along the way. Most people like you, many love you, and one or two think that you really are the best thing since sliced bread.

Aquarius with Virgo Ascendant

How could anyone make the convention unconventional? Well, if anyone can manage, you can. There are great contradictions here, because on the one hand you always want to do the expected thing, but the Aquarian quality within your nature loves to surprise everyone on the way. If you don't always know what you are thinking or doing, it's a pretty safe bet that others won't either, so it's important on occasions really to stop and think. However this is not a pressing concern, because you tend to live a fairly happy life and muddle through no matter what. Other people tend to take to you well and it is likely that you will have many friends. You tend to be bright and cheerful and can approach even difficult tasks with the certainty that you have the skills necessary to see them through to their conclusion. Give and take are important factors in the life of any individual and particularly so in your case. Because you can stretch yourself in order to understand what makes other people think and act in the way that they do, you have the reputation of being a good friend and a reliable colleague.

In love you can be somewhat more fickle than the typical Virgoan, and yet you are always interesting to live with. Where you are, things happen, and you mix a sparkling wit with deep insights.

Aquarius with Libra Ascendant

Stand by for a truly interesting and very inspiring combination here, but one that is sometimes rather difficult to fathom, even for the sort of people who believe themselves to be very perceptive. The reason for this could be that any situation has to be essentially fixed and constant in order to get a handle on it, and this is certainly not the case for the Aquarian–Libran type. The fact is that both these signs are Air signs, and to a certain extent as unpredictable as the wind itself.

To most people you seem to be original, frank, free and very outspoken. Not everything you do makes sense to others and if you were alive during the hippy era, it is likely that you went around with flowers in your hair, for you are a free-thinking idealist at heart. With age you mature somewhat, but never too much, because you will always see the strange, the comical and the original in life. This is what keeps you young and is one of the factors that makes you so very attractive to members of the opposite sex. Many people will want to 'adopt' you and you are at your very best when in company. Much of your effort is expounded on others and yet, unless you discipline yourself a good deal, personal relationships of the romantic sort can bring certain difficulties. Careful planning is necessary.

Aquarius with Scorpio Ascendant

Here we have a combination that shows much promise and a flexibility that allows many changes in direction, allied to a power to succeed, sometimes very much against all the odds. Aquarius lightens the load of the Scorpio mind, turning the depths into potential, and intuitive foresight into a means for getting on in life. There are depths here, because even airy Aquarius isn't so easy to understand, and it is therefore a fact that some people with this combination will always be something of a mystery. However, even this fact can be turned to your advantage because it means that people will always be looking at you. Confidence is so often the key to success in life and the Scorpio–Aquarius mix offers this, or at least appears to do so. Even when this is not entirely the case, the fact that everyone around you believes it to be true is often enough.

You are usually good to know, and show a keen intellect and a deep intelligence, aided by a fascination for life that knows no bounds. When at your best you are giving, understanding, balanced and active. On those occasions when things are not going well for you, beware of a stubborn streak and the need to be sensational. Keep it light and happy and you won't go far wrong. Most of you are very, very much loved.

Aquarius with Sagittarius Ascendant

There is an original streak to your nature which is very attractive to the people with whom you share your life. Always different, ever on the go and anxious to try out the next experiment in life, you are interested in almost everything, and yet deeply attached to almost nothing. Everyone you know thinks that you are a little 'odd', but you probably don't mind them believing this because you know it to be true. In fact it is possible that you positively relish your eccentricity, which sets you apart from the common herd and means that you are always going to be noticed.

Although it may seem strange with this combination of Air and Fire, you can be distinctly cool on occasions, have a deep and abiding love of your own company now and again and won't be easily understood. Love comes fairly easily to you but there are times when you are accused of being self-possessed, self-indulgent and not willing enough to fall in line with the wishes of those around you. Despite this you walk on and on down your own path. At heart you are an extrovert and you love to party, often late into the night. Luxury appeals to you, though it tends to be of the transient sort. Travel could easily play a major and a very important part in your life.

Aquarius with Capricorn Ascendant

Here the determination of Capricorn is assisted by a slightly more adaptable quality and an off-beat personality that tends to keep everyone else guessing. You don't care to be quite so predictable as the archetypal Capricorn would be, and there is a more idealistic quality here, or at least one that shows more. A greater number of friends than Capricorn usually keeps is likely, though less than the true Aquarian would gather. Few people doubt your sincerity, though by no means all of them understand what makes you tick. Unfortunately you are not in a position to help them out, because you are not too sure yourself. All the same, you muddle through and can be very capable when the mood takes you.

Being a natural traveller, you love to see new places and would be quite fascinated by cultures that are very different to your own. People with this combination are inclined to spend some time living abroad and may even settle there. You look out for the underdog and will always have time for a good cause, no matter what it takes to help. In romantic terms you are a reliable partner, though with a slightly wayward edge which, if anything, tends to make you even more attractive. Listen to your intuition, which is well honed and rarely lets you down. Generally speaking you are very popular.

THE MOON AND THE PART IT PLAYS IN YOUR LIFE

In astrology the Moon is probably the single most important heavenly body after the Sun. Its unique position, as partner to the Earth on its journey around the solar system, means that the Moon appears to pass through the signs of the zodiac extremely quickly. The zodiac position of the Moon at the time of your birth plays a great part in personal character and is especially significant in the build-up of your emotional nature.

Your Own Moon Sign

Discovering the position of the Moon at the time of your birth has always been notoriously difficult because tracking the complex zodiac positions of the Moon is not easy. This process has been reduced to three simple stages with our Lunar Tables. A breakdown of the Moon's zodiac positions can be found from page 35 onwards, so that once you know what your Moon Sign is, you can see what part this plays in the overall build-up of your personal character.

If you follow the instructions on the next page you will soon be able to work out exactly what zodiac sign the Moon occupied on the day that you were born and you can then go on to compare the reading for this position with those of your Sun sign and your Ascendant. It is partly the comparison between these three important positions that goes towards making you the unique individual you are.

HOW TO DISCOVER YOUR MOON SIGN

This is a three-stage process. You may need a pen and a piece of paper but if you follow the instructions below the process should only take a minute or so.

STAGE 1 First of all you need to know the Moon Age at the time of your birth. If you look at Moon Table 1, on page 33, you will find all the years between 1910 and 2008 down the left side. Find the year of your birth and then trace across to the right to the month of your birth. Where the two intersect you will find a number. This is the date of the New Moon in the month that you were born. You now need to count forward the number of days between the New Moon and your own birthday. For example, if the New Moon in the month of your birth was shown as being the 6th and you were born on the 20th, your Moon Age Day would be 14. If the New Moon in the month of your birth came after your birthday, you need to count forward from the New Moon in the previous month. If you were born in a Leap Year, remember to count the 29th February. You can tell if your birth year was a Leap Year if the last two digits can be divided by four. Whatever the result, jot this number down so that you do not forget it.

STAGE 2 Take a look at Moon Table 2 on page 34. Down the left hand column look for the date of your birth. Now trace across to the month of your birth. Where the two meet you will find a letter. Copy this letter down alongside your Moon Age Day.

STAGE 3 Moon Table 3 on page 34 will supply you with the zodiac sign the Moon occupied on the day of your birth. Look for your Moon Age Day down the left hand column and then for the letter you found in Stage 2. Where the two converge you will find a zodiac sign and this is the sign occupied by the Moon on the day that you were born.

Your Zodiac Moon Sign Explained

You will find a profile of all zodiac Moon Signs on pages 35 to 38, showing in yet another way how astrology helps to make you into the individual that you are. In each daily entry of the Astral Diary you can find the zodiac position of the Moon for every day of the year. This also allows you to discover your lunar birthdays. Since the Moon passes through all the signs of the zodiac in about a month, you can expect something like twelve lunar birthdays each year. At these times you are likely to be emotionally steady and able to make the sort of decisions that have real, lasting value.

MOON TABLE 1

YEAR	DEC	JAN	FEB	YEAR	DEC	JAN	FEB	YEAR	DEC	JAN	FEB
1910	1/30	11	9	1943	27	6	4	1976	21	1/31	29
1911	20	29	28	1944	15	25	24	1977	10	19	18
1912	9	18	17	1945	4	14	12	1978	29	9	7
1913	27	7	6	1946	23	3	2	1979	18	27	26
1914	17	25	24	1947	12	21	19	1980	7	16	15
1915	6	15	14	1948	1/30	11	9	1981	26	6	4
1916	25	5	3	1949	19	29	27	1982	15	25	23
1917	13	24	22	1950	9	18	16	1983	4	14	13
1918	2	12	11	1951	28	7	6	1984	22	3	1
1919	21	1/31	–	1952	17	26	25	1985	12	21	19
1920	10	20	19	1953	6	15	14	1986	1/30	10	9
1921	29	9	8	1954	25	5	3	1987	20	29	28
1922	18	27	26	1955	14	24	22	1988	9	19	17
1923	8	17	15	1956	2	13	11	1989	28	7	6
1924	26	6	5	1957	21	1/30	–	1990	17	26	25
1925	15	24	23	1958	10	19	18	1991	6	15	14
1926	5	14	12	1959	29	9	7	1992	24	4	3
1927	24	3	2	1960	18	27	26	1993	14	23	22
1928	12	21	19	1961	7	16	15	1994	2	11	10
1929	1/30	11	9	1962	26	6	5	1995	22	1/30	–
1930	19	29	28	1963	15	25	23	1996	10	20	18
1931	9	18	17	1964	4	14	13	1997	28	9	7
1932	27	7	6	1965	22	3	1	1998	18	27	26
1933	17	25	24	1966	12	21	19	1999	7	17	16
1934	6	15	14	1967	1/30	10	9	2000	26	6	4
1935	25	5	3	1968	20	29	28	2001	15	25	23
1936	13	24	22	1969	9	19	17	2002	4	13	12
1937	2	12	11	1970	28	7	6	2003	23	3	1
1938	21	1/31	–	1971	17	26	25	2004	11	21	20
1939	10	20	19	1972	6	15	14	2005	30	10	9
1940	28	9	8	1973	25	5	4	2006	20	29	28
1941	18	27	26	1974	14	24	22	2007	9	18	16
1942	8	16	15	1975	3	12	11	2008	27	8	6

TABLE 2   MOON TABLE 3

DAY	JAN	FEB	M/D	A	B	C	D	E	F	G
1	A	D	0	CP	AQ	AQ	AQ	PI	PI	PI
2	A	D	1	AQ	AQ	AQ	PI	PI	PI	AR
3	A	D	2	AQ	AQ	PI	PI	PI	AR	AR
4	A	D	3	AQ	PI	PI	PI	AR	AR	AR
5	A	D	4	PI	PI	AR	AR	AR	AR	TA
6	A	D	5	PI	AR	AR	AR	TA	TA	TA
7	A	D	6	AR	AR	AR	TA	TA	TA	GE
8	A	D	7	AR	AR	TA	TA	TA	GE	GE
9	A	D	8	AR	TA	TA	TA	GE	GE	GE
10	A	E	9	TA	TA	GE	GE	GE	CA	CA
11	B	E	10	TA	GE	GE	GE	CA	CA	CA
12	B	E	11	GE	GE	GE	CA	CA	CA	LE
13	B	E	12	GE	GE	CA	CA	CA	LE	LE
14	B	E	13	GE	CA	CA	LE	LE	LE	LE
15	B	E	14	CA	CA	LE	LE	LE	VI	VI
16	B	E	15	CA	LE	LE	LE	VI	VI	VI
17	B	E	16	LE	LE	LE	VI	VI	VI	LI
18	B	E	17	LE	LE	VI	VI	VI	LI	LI
19	B	E	18	LE	VI	VI	VI	LI	LI	LI
20	B	F	19	VI	VI	VI	LI	LI	LI	SC
21	C	F	20	VI	LI	LI	LI	SC	SC	SC
22	C	F	21	LI	LI	LI	SC	SC	SC	SA
23	C	F	22	LI	LI	SC	SC	SC	SA	SA
24	C	F	23	LI	SC	SC	SC	SA	SA	SA
25	C	F	24	SC	SC	SC	SA	SA	SA	CP
26	C	F	25	SC	SA	SA	SA	CP	CP	CP
27	C	F	26	SA	SA	SA	CP	CP	CP	AQ
28	C	F	27	SA	SA	CP	CP	AQ	AQ	AQ
29	C	F	28	SA	CP	CP	AQ	AQ	AQ	AQ
30	C	–	29	CP	CP	CP	AQ	AQ	AQ	PI
31	D	–								

AR = Aries, TA = Taurus, GE = Gemini, CA = Cancer, LE = Leo, VI = Virgo, LI = Libra, SC = Scorpio, SA = Sagittarius, CP = Capricorn, AQ = Aquarius, PI = Pisces

34

MOON SIGNS

Moon in Aries

You have a strong imagination, courage, determination and a desire to do things in your own way and forge your own path through life.

Originality is a key attribute; you are seldom stuck for ideas although your mind is changeable and you could take the time to focus on individual tasks. Often quick-tempered, you take orders from few people and live life at a fast pace. Avoid health problems by taking regular time out for rest and relaxation.

Emotionally, it is important that you talk to those you are closest to and work out your true feelings. Once you discover that people are there to help, there is less necessity for you to do everything yourself.

Moon in Taurus

The Moon in Taurus gives you a courteous and friendly manner, which means you are likely to have many friends.

The good things in life mean a lot to you, as Taurus is an Earth sign that delights in experiences which please the senses. Hence you are probably a lover of good food and drink, which may in turn mean you need to keep an eye on the bathroom scales, especially as looking good is also important to you.

Emotionally you are fairly stable and you stick by your own standards. Taureans do not respond well to change. Intuition also plays an important part in your life.

Moon in Gemini

You have a warm-hearted character, sympathetic and eager to help others. At times reserved, you can also be articulate and chatty: this is part of the paradox of Gemini, which always brings duplicity to the nature. You are interested in current affairs, have a good intellect, and are good company and likely to have many friends. Most of your friends have a high opinion of you and would be ready to defend you should the need arise. However, this is usually unnecessary, as you are quite capable of defending yourself in any verbal confrontation.

Travel is important to your inquisitive mind and you find intellectual stimulus in mixing with people from different cultures. You also gain much from reading, writing and the arts but you do need plenty of rest and relaxation in order to avoid fatigue.

Moon in Cancer

The Moon in Cancer at the time of birth is a fortunate position as Cancer is the Moon's natural home. This means that the qualities of compassion and understanding given by the Moon are especially enhanced in your nature, and you are friendly and sociable and cope well with emotional pressures. You cherish home and family life, and happily do the domestic tasks. Your surroundings are important to you and you hate squalor and filth. You are likely to have a love of music and poetry.

Your basic character, although at times changeable like the Moon itself, depends on symmetry. You aim to make your surroundings comfortable and harmonious, for yourself and those close to you.

Moon in Leo

The best qualities of the Moon and Leo come together to make you warm-hearted, fair, ambitious and self-confident. With good organisational abilities, you invariably rise to a position of responsibility in your chosen career. This is fortunate as you don't enjoy being an 'also-ran' and would rather be an important part of a small organisation than a menial in a large one.

You should be lucky in love, and happy, provided you put in the effort to make a comfortable home for yourself and those close to you. It is likely that you will have a love of pleasure, sport, music and literature. Life brings you many rewards, most of them as a direct result of your own efforts, although you may be luckier than average and ready to make the best of any situation.

Moon in Virgo

You are endowed with good mental abilities and a keen receptive memory, but you are never ostentatious or pretentious. Naturally quite reserved, you still have many friends, especially of the opposite sex. Marital relationships must be discussed carefully and worked at so that they remain harmonious, as personal attachments can be a problem if you do not give them your full attention.

Talented and persevering, you possess artistic qualities and are a good homemaker. Earning your honours through genuine merit, you work long and hard towards your objectives but show little pride in your achievements. Many short journeys will be undertaken in your life.

Moon in Libra

With the Moon in Libra you are naturally popular and make friends easily. People like you, probably more than you realise, you bring fun to a party and are a natural diplomat. For all its good points, Libra is not the most stable of astrological signs and, as a result, your emotions can be a little unstable too. Therefore, although the Moon in Libra is said to be good for love and marriage, your Sun sign and Rising sign will have an important effect on your emotional and loving qualities.

You must remember to relate to others in your decision-making. Co-operation is crucial because Libra represents the 'balance' of life that can only be achieved through harmonious relationships. Conformity is not easy for you because Libra, an Air sign, likes its independence.

Moon in Scorpio

Some people might call you pushy. In fact, all you really want to do is to live life to the full and protect yourself and your family from the pressures of life. Take care to avoid giving the impression of being sarcastic or impulsive and use your energies wisely and constructively.

You have great courage and you invariably achieve your goals by force of personality and sheer effort. You are fond of mystery and are good at predicting the outcome of situations and events. Travel experiences can be beneficial to you.

You may experience problems if you do not take time to examine your motives in a relationship, and also if you allow jealousy, always a feature of Scorpio, to cloud your judgement.

Moon in Sagittarius

The Moon in Sagittarius helps to make you a generous individual with humanitarian qualities and a kind heart. Restlessness may be intrinsic as your mind is seldom still. Perhaps because of this, you have a need for change that could lead you to several major moves during your adult life. You are not afraid to stand your ground when you know your judgement is right, you speak directly and have good intuition.

At work you are quick, efficient and versatile and so you make an ideal employee. You need work to be intellectually demanding and do not enjoy tedious routines.

In relationships, you anger quickly if faced with stupidity or deception, though you are just as quick to forgive and forget. Emotionally, there are times when your heart rules your head.

Moon in Capricorn

The Moon in Capricorn makes you popular and likely to come into the public eye in some way. The watery Moon is not entirely comfortable in the Earth sign of Capricorn and this may lead to some difficulties in the early years of life. An initial lack of creative ability and indecision must be overcome before the true qualities of patience and perseverance inherent in Capricorn can show through.

You have good administrative ability and are a capable worker, and if you are careful you can accumulate wealth. But you must be cautious and take professional advice in partnerships, as you are open to deception. You may be interested in social or welfare work, which suit your organisational skills and sympathy for others.

Moon in Aquarius

The Moon in Aquarius makes you an active and agreeable person with a friendly, easy-going nature. Sympathetic to the needs of others, you flourish in a laid-back atmosphere. You are broad-minded, fair and open to suggestion, although sometimes you have an unconventional quality which others can find hard to understand.

You are interested in the strange and curious, and in old articles and places. You enjoy trips to these places and gain much from them. Political, scientific and educational work interests you and you might choose a career in science or technology.

Money-wise, you make gains through innovation and concentration and Lunar Aquarians often tackle more than one job at a time. In love you are kind and honest.

Moon in Pisces

You have a kind, sympathetic nature, somewhat retiring at times, but you always take account of others' feelings and help when you can.

Personal relationships may be problematic, but as life goes on you can learn from your experiences and develop a better understanding of yourself and the world around you.

You have a fondness for travel, appreciate beauty and harmony and hate disorder and strife. You may be fond of literature and would make a good writer or speaker yourself. You have a creative imagination and may come across as an incurable romantic. You have strong intuition, maybe bordering on a mediumistic quality, which sets you apart from the mass. You may not be rich in cash terms, but your personal gifts are worth more than gold.

AQUARIUS IN LOVE

Discover how compatible in love you are with people from the same and other signs of the zodiac. Five stars equals a match made in heaven!

Aquarius meets Aquarius

This is a good match for several reasons. Most importantly, although it sounds arrogant, Aquarians like themselves. At its best, Aquarius is one of the fairest, most caring and genuinely pleasant zodiac signs and so it is only when faced by the difficulties created by others that it shows a less favourable side. Put two Aquarians together and voilà – instant success! Personal and family life should bring more joy. On the whole, a platform for adventure based on solid foundations. Star rating: *****

Aquarius meets Pisces

Zodiac signs that follow each other often have something in common, but this is not the case with Aquarius and Pisces. Both signs are deeply caring, but in different ways. Pisces is one of the deepest zodiac signs, and Aquarius simply isn't prepared to embark on the journey. Pisceans, meanwhile, would probably find Aquarians superficial and even flippant. On the positive side there is potential for a well-balanced relationship, but unless one party is untypical of their zodiac sign, it often doesn't get started. Star rating: **

Aquarius meets Aries

Aquarius is an Air sign, and Air and Fire often work well together, but not in the case of Aries and Aquarius. The average Aquarian lives in what the Ram sees as a fantasy world, so a meeting of minds is unlikely. Of course, the dominant side of Aries could be trained by the devil-may-care attitude of Aquarius. There are meeting points but they are difficult to establish. However, given sufficient time and an open mind on both sides, a degree of happiness is possible. Star rating: **

Aquarius meets Taurus

In any relationship of which Aquarius is a part, surprises abound. It is difficult for Taurus to understand the soul-searching, adventurous, changeable Aquarian, but on the positive side, the Bull is adaptable and can respond well to a dose of excitement. Aquarians are kind and react well to the same quality coming back at them. Both are friendly, capable of deep affection and basically creative. Unfortunately, Taurus simply doesn't know what makes Aquarius tick, which could lead to feelings of isolation, even if these don't always show on the surface. Star rating: **

Aquarius meets Gemini

Aquarius is commonly mistaken for a Water sign, but in fact it's ruled by the Air element, and this is the key to its compatibility with Gemini. Both signs mix freely socially, and each has an insatiable curiosity. There is plenty of action, lots of love, but very little rest, and so great potential for success if they don't wear each other out! Aquarius revels in its own eccentricity, and encourages Gemini to emulate this. Theirs will be an unconventional household, but almost everyone warms to this crazy and unpredictable couple. Star rating: *****

Aquarius meets Cancer

Cancer is often attracted to Aquarius and, as Aquarius is automatically on the side of anyone who fancies it, so there is the potential for something good here. Cancer loves Aquarius' devil-may-care approach to life, but also recognises and seeks to strengthen the basic lack of self-confidence that all Air signs try so hard to keep secret. Both signs are natural travellers and are quite adventurous. Their family life could be unusual, but friends would recognise a caring, sharing household with many different interests shared by people genuinely in love. Star rating: ***

Aquarius meets Leo

The problem here is that Aquarius doesn't think in the general sense of the word, it knows. Leo, on the other hand, is more practical and relies more on logical reasoning, and consequently it doesn't understand Aquarius very well. Aquarians can also appear slightly frosty in their appreciation of others and this, too, will annoy Leo. This is a good match for a business partnership because Aquarius is astute, while Leo is brave, but personally the prognosis is less promising. Tolerance, understanding and forbearance are all needed to make this work. Star rating: **

Aquarius meets Virgo

Aquarius is a strange sign because no matter how well one knows it, it always manages to surprise. For this reason, against the odds, it's quite likely that Aquarius will form a sucessful relationship with Virgo. Aquarius is changeable, unpredictable and often quite odd, while Virgo is steady, a fuss-pot and very practical. Herein lies the key. What one sign needs, the other provides and that may be the surest recipe for success imaginable. On-lookers may not know why the couple are happy, but they will recognise that this is the case. Star rating: ****

Aquarius meets Libra

One of the best combinations imaginable, partly because both are Air signs and so share a common meeting point. But perhaps the more crucial factor is that both signs respect each other. Aquarius loves life and originality, and is quite intellectual. Libra is similar, but more balanced and rather less eccentric. A visit to this couple's house would be entertaining and full of zany wit, activity and excitement. Both are keen to travel and may prefer to 'find themselves' before taking on too many domestic responsibilities. Star rating: *****

Aquarius meets Scorpio

This is a promising and practical combination. Scorpio responds well to Aquarius' persistent exploration of its deep nature and so this generally shy sign becomes lighter, brighter and more inspirational. Meanwhile, Aquarians are rarely as sure of themselves as they like to appear and are reassured by Scorpio's constant, steady and determined support. Both signs want to be kind to each other, which is a good starting point to a relationship that should be warm most of the time and extremely hot occasionally. Star rating: ****

Aquarius meets Sagittarius

Both Sagittarius and Aquarius are into mind games, which may lead to something of an intellectual competition. If one side is happy to be 'bamboozled' it won't be a problem, but it is more likely that the relationship will turn into a competition, which won't auger well for its long-term future. However, on the plus side, both signs are adventurous and sociable, so as long as there is always something new and interesting to do, the match could turn out very well. Star rating: **

Aquarius meets Capricorn

Probably one of the least likely combinations, as Capricorn and Aquarius are unlikely to choose each other in the first place, unless one side is quite untypical of their sign. Capricorn approaches things in a practical way and likes to get things done, while Aquarius works almost exclusively for the moment and relies heavily on intuition. Their attitudes to romance are also diametrically opposed: Aquarius' moods tend to swing from red hot to ice cold in a minute, which is alien to steady Capricorn. Star rating: **

VENUS:
THE PLANET OF LOVE

If you look up at the sky around sunset or sunrise you will often see Venus in close attendance to the Sun. It is arguably one of the most beautiful sights of all and there is little wonder that historically it became associated with the goddess of love. But although Venus does play an important part in the way you view love and in the way others see you romantically, this is only one of the spheres of influence that it enjoys in your overall character.

Venus has a part to play in the more cultured side of your life and has much to do with your appreciation of art, literature, music and general creativity. Even the way you look is responsive to the part of the zodiac that Venus occupied at the start of your life, though this fact is also down to your Sun sign and Ascending sign. If, at the time you were born, Venus occupied one of the more gregarious zodiac signs, you will be more likely to wear your heart on your sleeve, as well as to be more attracted to entertainment, social gatherings and good company. If on the other hand Venus occupied a quiet zodiac sign at the time of your birth, you would tend to be more retiring and less willing to shine in public situations.

It's good to know what part the planet Venus plays in your life for it can have a great bearing on the way you appear to the rest of the world and since we all have to mix with others, you can learn to make the very best of what Venus has to offer you.

One of the great complications in the past has always been trying to establish exactly what zodiac position Venus enjoyed when you were born because the planet is notoriously difficult to track. However, we have solved that problem by creating a table that is exclusive to your Sun sign, which you will find on the following page.

Establishing your Venus sign could not be easier. Just look up the year of your birth on the following page and you will see a sign of the zodiac. This was the sign that Venus occupied in the period covered by your sign in that year. If Venus occupied more than one sign during the period, this is indicated by the date on which the sign changed, and the name of the new sign. For instance, if you were born in 1945, Venus was in Pisces until the 12th February, after which time it was in Aries. If you were born before 12th February your Venus sign is Pisces, if you were born on or after 12th February, your Venus sign is Aries. Once you have established the position of Venus at the time of your birth, you can then look in the pages which follow to see how this has a bearing on your life as a whole.

1910 AQUARIUS
1911 AQUARIUS / 3.2 PISCES
1912 SAGITTARIUS / 30.1 CAPRICORN
1913 PISCES / 16.2 ARIES
1914 CAPRICORN / 26.1 AQUARIUS / 19.2 PISCES
1915 SAGITTARIUS / 7.2 CAPRICORN
1916 PISCES / 14.2 ARIES
1917 CAPRICORN / 9.2 AQUARIUS
1918 AQUARIUS
1919 AQUARIUS / 3.2 PISCES
1920 SAGITTARIUS / 30.1 CAPRICORN
1921 PISCES / 15.2 ARIES
1922 CAPRICORN / 25.1 AQUARIUS / 18.2 PISCES
1923 SAGITTARIUS / 7.2 CAPRICORN
1924 PISCES / 13.2 ARIES
1925 CAPRICORN / 9.2 AQUARIUS
1926 AQUARIUS
1927 AQUARIUS / 2.2 PISCES
1928 SAGITTARIUS / 29.1 CAPRICORN
1929 PISCES / 14.2 ARIES
1930 CAPRICORN / 25.1 AQUARIUS / 18.2 PISCES
1931 SAGITTARIUS / 6.2 CAPRICORN
1932 PISCES / 13.2 ARIES
1933 CAPRICORN / 8.2 AQUARIUS
1934 AQUARIUS
1935 AQUARIUS / 2.2 PISCES
1936 SAGITTARIUS / 29.1 CAPRICORN
1937 PISCES / 13.2 ARIES
1938 CAPRICORN / 24.1 AQUARIUS / 17.2 PISCES
1939 SAGITTARIUS / 6.2 CAPRICORN
1940 PISCES / 12.2 ARIES
1941 CAPRICORN / 8.2 AQUARIUS
1942 AQUARIUS
1943 AQUARIUS / 1.2 PISCES
1944 SAGITTARIUS / 28.1 CAPRICORN
1945 PISCES / 12.2 ARIES
1946 CAPRICORN / 24.1 AQUARIUS / 17.2 PISCES
1947 SAGITTARIUS / 6.2 CAPRICORN
1948 PISCES / 12.2 ARIES
1949 CAPRICORN / 7.2 AQUARIUS
1950 AQUARIUS
1951 AQUARIUS / 1.2 PISCES
1952 SAGITTARIUS / 27.1 CAPRICORN
1953 PISCES / 11.2 ARIES
1954 CAPRICORN / 23.1 AQUARIUS / 16.2 PISCES
1955 SAGITTARIUS / 6.2 CAPRICORN
1956 PISCES / 11.2 ARIES
1957 CAPRICORN / 7.2 AQUARIUS
1958 AQUARIUS
1959 AQUARIUS / 31.1 PISCES
1960 SAGITTARIUS / 27.1 CAPRICORN

1961 PISCES / 9.2 ARIES
1962 CAPRICORN / 23.1 AQUARIUS / 15.2 PISCES
1963 SAGITTARIUS / 6.2 CAPRICORN
1964 PISCES / 11.2 ARIES
1965 CAPRICORN / 6.2 AQUARIUS
1966 AQUARIUS
1967 AQUARIUS / 30.1 PISCES
1968 SAGITTARIUS / 26.1 CAPRICORN
1969 PISCES / 7.2 ARIES
1970 CAPRICORN / 22.1 AQUARIUS / 15.2 PISCES
1971 SAGITTARIUS / 5.2 CAPRICORN
1972 PISCES / 10.2 ARIES
1973 CAPRICORN / 5.2 AQUARIUS
1974 AQUARIUS / 7.2 CAPRICORN
1975 AQUARIUS / 30.1 PISCES
1976 SAGITTARIUS / 26.1 CAPRICORN
1977 PISCES / 5.2 ARIES
1978 CAPRICORN / 22.1 AQUARIUS / 14.2 PISCES
1979 SAGITTARIUS / 5.2 CAPRICORN
1980 PISCES / 10.2 ARIES
1981 CAPRICORN / 5.2 AQUARIUS
1982 AQUARIUS / 29.1 CAPRICORN
1983 AQUARIUS / 29.1 PISCES
1984 SAGITTARIUS / 25.1 CAPRICORN
1985 PISCES / 5.2 ARIES
1986 AQUARIUS / 14.2 PISCES
1987 SAGITTARIUS / 5.2 CAPRICORN
1988 PISCES / 9.2 ARIES
1989 CAPRICORN / 4.2 AQUARIUS
1990 AQUARIUS / 23.1 CAPRICORN
1991 AQUARIUS / 29.1 PISCES
1992 SAGITTARIUS / 25.1 CAPRICORN
1993 PISCES / 4.2 ARIES
1994 AQUARIUS / 13.2 PISCES
1995 SAGITTARIUS / 5.2 CAPRICORN
1996 PISCES / 9.2 ARIES
1997 CAPRICORN / 4.2 AQUARIUS
1998 AQUARIUS / 23.1 CAPRICORN
1999 AQUARIUS / 29.1 PISCES
2000 SAGITTARIUS / 25.1 CAPRICORN
2001 PISCES / 4.2 ARIES
2002 AQUARIUS / 13.2 PISCES
2003 SAGITTARIUS
2004 PISCES / 9.2 AQUARIUS
2005 CAPRICORN / 6.2 AQUARIUS
2006 AQUARIUS / 14.01 CAPRICORN
2007 AQUARIUS / 19.01 PISCES
2008 SAGITTARIUS / 25.1 CAPRICORN

VENUS THROUGH THE ZODIAC SIGNS

Venus in Aries

Amongst other things, the position of Venus in Aries indicates a fondness for travel, music and all creative pursuits. Your nature tends to be affectionate and you would try not to create confusion or difficulty for others if it could be avoided. Many people with this planetary position have a great love of the theatre, and mental stimulation is of the greatest importance. Early romantic attachments are common with Venus in Aries, so it is very important to establish a genuine sense of romantic continuity. Early marriage is not recommended, especially if it is based on sympathy. You may give your heart a little too readily on occasions.

Venus in Taurus

You are capable of very deep feelings and your emotions tend to last for a very long time. This makes you a trusting partner and lover, whose constancy is second to none. In life you are precise and careful and always try to do things the right way. Although this means an ordered life, which you are comfortable with, it can also lead you to be rather too fussy for your own good. Despite your pleasant nature, you are very fixed in your opinions and quite able to speak your mind. Others are attracted to you and historical astrologers always quoted this position of Venus as being very fortunate in terms of marriage. However, if you find yourself involved in a failed relationship, it could take you a long time to trust again.

Venus in Gemini

As with all associations related to Gemini, you tend to be quite versatile, anxious for change and intelligent in your dealings with the world at large. You may gain money from more than one source but you are equally good at spending it. There is an inference here that you are a good communicator, via either the written or the spoken word, and you love to be in the company of interesting people. Always on the look-out for culture, you may also be very fond of music, and love to indulge the curious and cultured side of your nature. In romance you tend to have more than one relationship and could find yourself associated with someone who has previously been a friend or even a distant relative.

Venus in Cancer

You often stay close to home because you are very fond of family and enjoy many of your most treasured moments when you are with those you love. Being naturally sympathetic, you will always do anything you can to support those around you, even people you hardly know at all. This charitable side of your nature is your most noticeable trait and is one of the reasons why others are naturally so fond of you. Being receptive and in some cases even psychic, you can see through to the soul of most of those with whom you come into contact. You may not commence too many romantic attachments but when you do give your heart, it tends to be unconditionally.

Venus in Leo

It must become quickly obvious to almost anyone you meet that you are kind, sympathetic and yet determined enough to stand up for anyone or anything that is truly important to you. Bright and sunny, you warm the world with your natural enthusiasm and would rarely do anything to hurt those around you, or at least not intentionally. In romance you are ardent and sincere, though some may find your style just a little overpowering. Gains come through your contacts with other people and this could be especially true with regard to romance, for love and money often come hand in hand for those who were born with Venus in Leo. People claim to understand you, though you are more complex than you seem.

Venus in Virgo

Your nature could well be fairly quiet no matter what your Sun sign might be, though this fact often manifests itself as an inner peace and would not prevent you from being basically sociable. Some delays and even the odd disappointment in love cannot be ruled out with this planetary position, though it's a fact that you will usually find the happiness you look for in the end. Catapulting yourself into romantic entanglements that you know to be rather ill-advised is not sensible, and it would be better to wait before you committed yourself exclusively to any one person. It is the essence of your nature to serve the world at large and through doing so it is possible that you will attract money at some stage in your life.

Venus in Libra

Venus is very comfortable in Libra and bestows upon those people who have this planetary position a particular sort of kindness that is easy to recognise. This is a very good position for all sorts of friendships and also for romantic attachments that usually bring much joy into your life. Few individuals with Venus in Libra would avoid marriage and since you are capable of great depths of love, it is likely that you will find a contented personal life. You like to mix with people of integrity and intelligence but don't take kindly to scruffy surroundings or work that means getting your hands too dirty. Careful speculation, good business dealings and money through marriage all seem fairly likely.

Venus in Scorpio

You are quite open and tend to spend money quite freely, even on those occasions when you don't have very much. Although your intentions are always good, there are times when you get yourself in to the odd scrape and this can be particularly true when it comes to romance, which you may come to late or from a rather unexpected direction. Certainly you have the power to be happy and to make others contented on the way, but you find the odd stumbling block on your journey through life and it could seem that you have to work harder than those around you. As a result of this, you gain a much deeper understanding of the true value of personal happiness than many people ever do, and are likely to achieve true contentment in the end.

Venus in Sagittarius

You are lighthearted, cheerful and always able to see the funny side of any situation. These facts enhance your popularity, which is especially high with members of the opposite sex. You should never have to look too far to find romantic interest in your life, though it is just possible that you might be too willing to commit yourself before you are certain that the person in question is right for you. Part of the problem here extends to other areas of life too. The fact is that you like variety in everything and so can tire of situations that fail to offer it. All the same, if you choose wisely and learn to understand your restless side, then great happiness can be yours.

Venus in Capricorn

The most notable trait that comes from Venus in this position is that it makes you trustworthy and able to take on all sorts of responsibilities in life. People are instinctively fond of you and love you all the more because you are always ready to help those who are in any form of need. Social and business popularity can be yours and there is a magnetic quality to your nature that is particularly attractive in a romantic sense. Anyone who wants a partner for a lover, a spouse and a good friend too would almost certainly look in your direction. Constancy is the hallmark of your nature and unfaithfulness would go right against the grain. You might sometimes be a little too trusting.

Venus in Aquarius

This location of Venus offers a fondness for travel and a desire to try out something new at every possible opportunity. You are extremely easy to get along with and tend to have many friends from varied backgrounds, classes and inclinations. You like to live a distinct sort of life and gain a great deal from moving about, both in a career sense and with regard to your home. It is not out of the question that you could form a romantic attachment to someone who comes from far away or be attracted to a person of a distinctly artistic and original nature. What you cannot stand is jealousy, for you have friends of both sexes and would want to keep things that way.

Venus in Pisces

The first thing people tend to notice about you is your wonderful, warm smile. Being very charitable by nature you will do anything to help others, even if you don't know them well. Much of your life may be spent sorting out situations for other people, but it is very important to feel that you are living for yourself too. In the main, you remain cheerful, and tend to be quite attractive to members of the opposite sex. Where romantic attachments are concerned, you could be drawn to people who are significantly older or younger than yourself or to someone with a unique career or point of view. It might be best for you to avoid marrying whilst you are still very young.

AQUARIUS:
2007 DIARY PAGES

October

2007

1 MONDAY
Moon Age Day 19   Moon Sign Gemini

New information can help you to be fully in the picture today and allows you to make progress in many different areas of your life. However, much of what stands around you is only potential, and much depends on your own efforts. Fortunately there are some very supportive planetary influences around this week.

2 TUESDAY
Moon Age Day 20   Moon Sign Gemini

It would be good to spread your influence socially and there is certainly no need to fall out with anyone, even though you might be quite touchy on occasions. Social trends remain generally positive, though you may decide to turn more and more to family members in order to fill your quiet hours at present.

3 WEDNESDAY
Moon Age Day 21   Moon Sign Cancer

Work and career issues have potential to keep you on the go now, in fact there may not be enough time to do everything that you would wish. Today responds best if you keep an open mind when it comes to changes that are now on the cards and don't spend too much time worrying about what might happen. Most decisions will be yours to make.

4 THURSDAY
Moon Age Day 22   Moon Sign Cancer

A day to keep your mind sharp and to make sure you know what you want at the moment. You can afford to speak your mind and leave few people in any doubt about your intentions. As the day grows older you may notice that you are growing quieter and more in need of moments for reflection.

5 FRIDAY
Moon Age Day 23   Moon Sign Leo

Only moderate advancement is indicated today. With the Moon in your solar sixth house the lunar low has arrived. Allow yourself moments of reflection and spend time with loved ones, particularly those who have a need of you at present. This might be a fairly quiet sort of Friday by your usual standards.

6 SATURDAY
Moon Age Day 24   Moon Sign Leo

You can expect a mixed bag this weekend. Although the lunar low might seem to be putting pressure on you in one way or another, there are sufficient positive aspects around today to help you to overcome its worst influences. In particular you have scope to revel in the company of people you find to be intelligent and stimulating.

7 SUNDAY
Moon Age Day 25   Moon Sign Leo

The Moon is still in Leo, though its influence there is waning significantly, and if there are any problems around today you can deal with them quickly and efficiently. Romance is an important factor in the lives of many Aquarians at the moment, with the position of the planet Venus offering a real boost to affairs of the heart.

8 MONDAY
Moon Age Day 26   Moon Sign Virgo

There may be some important things to do today, though they might not turn out to be quite as simple as you might wish. Still, it is possible to apply a little concentration, just as long as you don't try to tackle too many tasks at the same time. Communication counts for a great deal later in the day.

9 TUESDAY
Moon Age Day 27   Moon Sign Virgo

Restlessness is possible today, but if you are wise you can turn it to your advantage. When it comes to discussions or arguments you might decide to back down, either because you recognise it is not in your best interests to question someone or simply because you want a simple life.

10 WEDNESDAY   *Moon Age Day 28   Moon Sign Libra*

Today marks a potentially busy time when you can still find moments for contemplation and for getting your head round problems that might have been with you for a while. Even casual conversations can offer significant clues as to your way forward in a practical sense, and meanwhile you could find love to be inviting.

11 THURSDAY   *Moon Age Day 0   Moon Sign Libra*

It would be better by far today to do what you have to do in your own way. Inventing new ways of going about tasks you already understand could well lead to problems further down the line. Your communication skills are certainly not in doubt and your intuition works to your advantage if you listen to it.

12 FRIDAY   ☿   *Moon Age Day 1   Moon Sign Libra*

Along comes an influx of social invitations and some of these could detract from your ability to concentrate on strictly practical matters when they matter the most. Never mind, you can make this an interesting period all the same, and being an Aquarian you can make the most of the stimulus that comes from interacting with others.

13 SATURDAY   ☿   *Moon Age Day 2   Moon Sign Scorpio*

Saturday offers you scope to make contact with types who can be of specific use to you practically, though by later in the day you may well be opting for fun. You won't be able to take anyone quite as seriously as would sometimes be the case and this even includes yourself.

14 SUNDAY   ☿   *Moon Age Day 3   Moon Sign Scorpio*

Trends encourage you to get more involved in domestic matters than has been possible for a week or so. You can turn your mind towards the needs that loved ones have of you and use much of your spare time to make others feel more secure. Don't be afraid to leave a few moments just for yourself and take some time out to meditate.

15 MONDAY ☿ *Moon Age Day 4   Moon Sign Sagittarius*

Finding the best qualities in others is quite natural to you, though it is a quality that is much enhanced right now. You have what it takes to turn heads and should also notice how much influence you have on those who are in positions of authority. You get your own way best now by using persuasion and not by arguing.

16 TUESDAY ☿ *Moon Age Day 5   Moon Sign Sagittarius*

In terms of money you can take advantage of a fairly stable period and one that will allow you to deal with financial matters in a positive way. The real prospects for gain seem to be at work, and you have all it takes to make a good impression. You needn't let any limitations be placed upon you at the moment.

17 WEDNESDAY ☿ *Moon Age Day 6   Moon Sign Sagittarius*

Even if there is plenty in the practical world to demand your attention, you could also be quite restless and anxious to ring the changes whenever you can. Friendship proves important at this stage and you have scope to turn to your best pals in order to get information that will help you to move forward.

18 THURSDAY ☿ *Moon Age Day 7   Moon Sign Capricorn*

You can be extremely persuasive under present planetary trends and should have very little difficulty persuading others to follow your lead. This can be especially useful at work, where you can use it to put yourself in the running for advancement of some sort. The world tends to be the way you make it right now, so think big!

19 FRIDAY ☿ *Moon Age Day 8   Moon Sign Capricorn*

Things will probably slow just a little as the Moon finishes its pass through your solar twelfth house. This is invariably a time during which you can withdraw somewhat, though you may not be quiet as the day advances and the Moon moves closer to your own zodiac sign of Aquarius.

20 SATURDAY ☿ *Moon Age Day 9*   *Moon Sign Aquarius*

New starts are there for the taking as the Moon races back into your own zodiac sign, from where it offers better luck, a very positive attitude and much assistance from others. Gains are possible financially and personally, even if you have to look around carefully in order to recognise one or two of them.

21 SUNDAY ☿ *Moon Age Day 10*   *Moon Sign Aquarius*

You have what it takes to remain ahead of the game most of the time and shouldn't have any real difficulty getting others to do what you think is best. With silver-tongued eloquence you prove just how wonderful the average Aquarian can be at getting his or her own way, and can also capitalise on some particularly good news.

22 MONDAY ☿   *Moon Age Day 11*   *Moon Sign Pisces*

Trends remain positive for you in a social sense now, and getting on with people who were difficult a few days ago should be quite easy. If routines are tiresome, your best approach is to ignore them if you can. Artistically you should be on top form and may decide this is a good time for planning changes at home.

23 TUESDAY ☿   *Moon Age Day 12*   *Moon Sign Pisces*

Perhaps you should not expect everything in life to suit you today, though the majority of situations should work out fine. Routines might be somewhat hard to establish and as is so often the case for you, there is a great temptation to throw the instruction book out of the window and to 'wing it'.

24 WEDNESDAY ☿   *Moon Age Day 13*   *Moon Sign Pisces*

There is one specific piece of advice that really matters today: get organised! You really do need to be on the ball and to prove to everyone around you that you know what you are doing and that you have a plan. Once people see that you are not simply bluffing your way through situations, co-operation should be assured.

25 THURSDAY ☿ *Moon Age Day 14   Moon Sign Aries*

As is so often the case for Aquarius it is very important to keep your eyes open and to make the most of information that comes your way. Getting an early start would help a great deal, particularly if there is a lot to get done. Tackling half a dozen jobs at the same time is no real drawback as far as you are concerned.

26 FRIDAY ☿ *Moon Age Day 15   Moon Sign Aries*

Intimate relationships offer promising moments and should help you to end the working week in a very favourable way. You have what it takes to win hearts and so if there is someone around you have been wishing to sweep off their feet, it seems as though this would be the best time of all to give it a go.

27 SATURDAY ☿ *Moon Age Day 16   Moon Sign Taurus*

This is a time to show your ingenious nature working at its best. Socially speaking you can enjoy a fairly easy-going sort of weekend and may not wish to be involved in lengthy or deep conversations of any sort. Proving what a party animal you are shouldn't be difficult, because you can enliven any event.

28 SUNDAY ☿ *Moon Age Day 17   Moon Sign Taurus*

You need to keep things varied today. The more change and diversity you get into your life, the better you are likely to enjoy what this Sunday has to offer. Why not leave all serious issues until another day and show how spontaneous you can be? You can also gain by simply being in the right place at the best time.

29 MONDAY ☿ *Moon Age Day 18   Moon Sign Gemini*

You would be wise to keep emotional issues at arm's length for the moment and avoid getting bogged down with serious discussions. You have scope to keep life light and airy and that is certainly the best way forward for you at present. Creative potential is good and so is your ability to find new ways to tackle jobs you have been doing for years.

30 TUESDAY ☿ *Moon Age Day 19   Moon Sign Gemini*

Even if it isn't always easy today to see a point of view you basically don't understand, it's only a matter of time before explanations are available. It is probable that there are some happenings taking place right now to which you cannot be a party for the moment. Try to curb your natural curiosity a little.

31 WEDNESDAY ☿ *Moon Age Day 20   Moon Sign Cancer*

You may find yourself having to be content with only moderate success in a practical or work sense, but once the responsibility is out of the way you should discover a day that is potentially rewarding. Romance is beginning to show more clearly in the Aquarian life and there are also rewards available as a result of past efforts.

November

2007

1 THURSDAY ☿ *Moon Age Day 21 Moon Sign Cancer*

There are signs that the first day of November could find you somewhat grumpy. The fact that the year is advancing so fast and in fact has nearly reached its end is hardly likely to inspire you. This is probably because you expect so much of yourself that it would be almost impossible to have everything you would wish.

2 FRIDAY ☿ *Moon Age Day 22 Moon Sign Leo*

With the lunar low present this would hardly be the best time for taking any sort of risk. In the main your best approach is to keep a generally low profile and to be content with your own company for at least part of the time. All Aquarians can use today as a significantly quieter interlude than would normally be the case.

3 SATURDAY *Moon Age Day 23 Moon Sign Leo*

Getting what you want most is possible today, though you would have to work so hard to achieve your objectives that you would exhaust yourself. On the other hand, you do have what it takes to get others to do things on your behalf. They think they are working towards their own objectives – but you, of course, know different!

4 SUNDAY *Moon Age Day 24 Moon Sign Virgo*

Look out for new friendships on the horizon, a fact that may well please you at a time when present attachments might be in doubt. Don't be too worried if you can't get family members to follow your instructions today. It's worth leaving them to their own devices and getting on with what is important to you, now the lunar low is out of the way.

5 MONDAY
Moon Age Day 25   Moon Sign Virgo

You can make the most of a little luck in the financial sphere around this time, and you need to be on the ball when it comes to any sort of deal that is in the offing. Look out for the odd practical mishap that is maybe caused because you are a little clumsier than would usually be the case.

6 TUESDAY
Moon Age Day 26   Moon Sign Libra

Even if those with whom you associated regularly think you are the bee's knees, this may not be universally true. Don't be downhearted about this, because you can't please everyone, and you need to be the sort of person you really are. When it matters the most you can persuade people to come good for you.

7 WEDNESDAY
Moon Age Day 27   Moon Sign Libra

A day to take a little trip if possible and to make some changes to the routines of your life. It would be all too easy to become bored with things at the moment, and in order to avoid this happening you may have to put in a little extra effort. Consideration for family members counts for a great deal now.

8 THURSDAY
Moon Age Day 28   Moon Sign Libra

It looks as though you have some big ideas now, and you need to do all you can to exploit them. In order to have things running the way you would really wish it might be necessary to get others to do your bidding. The more diplomatic you show yourself to be today, the greater is the chance that they will help.

9 FRIDAY
Moon Age Day 0   Moon Sign Scorpio

This has potential to be a very split sort of day. Mercury encourages your communicative side, but other planetary influences show that there is also a quieter aspect to your nature. One area of life that should be looking fairly good is romance – so much so that a new attachment is a possibility for some Aquarians.

10 SATURDAY   *Moon Age Day 1   Moon Sign Scorpio*

You have scope to get out and about more than ever today and the weekend offers much to those Aquarians who are genuinely willing to put themselves out. There isn't any use in waiting around for anyone else to make the arrangements, and although you will have to work hard to get others involved, the effort should be more than worthwhile.

11 SUNDAY   *Moon Age Day 2   Moon Sign Sagittarius*

This would be a very favourable time for all matters to do with holiday arrangements or even for planning a business trip of some sort. There is a degree of restlessness about you at this time and you need to bring some change into your life if you are not to end up feeling rather bored.

12 MONDAY   *Moon Age Day 3   Moon Sign Sagittarius*

Communication with others can be enlivening and even exciting at the start of this new working week. You tend to be acting on impulse for much of the time, but this is so much a part of your basic nature that it isn't any sort of problem. Be prepared to listen to the ideas of a colleague because they could suit you too.

13 TUESDAY   *Moon Age Day 4   Moon Sign Sagittarius*

Today responds best if you take every possible opportunity to get away from the ordinary in life. Winter is here and things can start to look very grey and uninspiring unless you put in that extra bit of effort yourself. Aquarius has the power to lift its own spirits and those of everyone with whom it comes into contact.

14 WEDNESDAY   *Moon Age Day 5   Moon Sign Capricorn*

Today can be favourable for career progress, but now that the Moon has entered your solar twelfth house you can also afford to take some time for necessary reflection. In a day or two things could get busy so you may as well take a short break from self-imposed pressure whilst you can.

15 THURSDAY   *Moon Age Day 6   Moon Sign Capricorn*

You remain basically optimistic and quite committed to the future, though there could be the odd setback today, and you will need to keep your wits about you if you if you don't want to start again at the beginning with some specific projects. It may be best to settle for a fairly steady day, but that might be too much to expect.

16 FRIDAY   *Moon Age Day 7   Moon Sign Aquarius*

Just as you were starting to flag a little, along comes the lunar high. There is tremendous incentive to get on with new ideas and schemes and to push forward progressively in most spheres of your life. What you definitely do have right now is popularity, and you could hardly fail to realise the fact.

17 SATURDAY   *Moon Age Day 8   Moon Sign Aquarius*

You can make this a really good weekend, and with the lunar high pushing from behind you have everything you need to move forward at a significant pace, no matter what you decide to do. Excitement is like food and drink to you at the moment and you need to find something to do that gives you a definite thrill.

18 SUNDAY   *Moon Age Day 9   Moon Sign Aquarius*

Keep up the pressure to have a good time and to take others along with you. Your company is inspiring and you can make sure you are the star of the show. There may be one or two people who don't think you are quite so wonderful, but that is part of the price paid by all Air-sign individuals such as you.

19 MONDAY   *Moon Age Day 10   Moon Sign Pisces*

Learning new things can be a great deal of fun this week and you can afford to launch yourself into projects with a great deal of enthusiasm. If certain people prove to be difficult, you will have to show great diplomacy if you are to avoid getting into some sort of disagreement or even a downright row.

20 TUESDAY
Moon Age Day 11   Moon Sign Pisces

Don't hesitate today. Things work best for you when you are willing to recognise a challenge and to face up to it immediately. There are definite gains to be made and some of these may be of a financial nature. Routines are out at the moment, partly because you won't have time for them.

21 WEDNESDAY
Moon Age Day 12   Moon Sign Aries

It is possible that you will be somewhat argumentative today, and you need to curb this tendency if you want to avoid falling out with someone who is in a position to do you a great deal of good. Count to ten before you react, and even when you are faced with people you see as being deliberately stupid you need to keep your cool.

22 THURSDAY
Moon Age Day 13   Moon Sign Aries

Conversations are good for you today, and now that you can be slightly less contentious than you were yesterday you can get a lot from them. Aquarius tends to act on impulse for much of the time and it looks as though today will be no exception. Why not save some time in the evening to please your partner?

23 FRIDAY
Moon Age Day 14   Moon Sign Taurus

This should prove to be one of the better days of the month during which to enjoy friendship and the simple things of life. If you feel a bit lacking in lustre all you probably need is a temporary change of scene. When a particular task gets boring or frustrating, don't be afraid to put it aside for a while.

24 SATURDAY
Moon Age Day 15   Moon Sign Taurus

Aquarians who work at the weekend should find today to be very useful, but even if your time is your own you shouldn't have any trouble filling it. Now is the time to get in step with friends and do something quite out of the ordinary if you can. Your worst enemy at the moment is boredom, and you need to be inventive to avoid it.

25 SUNDAY   *Moon Age Day 16   Moon Sign Gemini*

Family and domestic situations are highlighted today. It's worth getting together with your loved ones and making some plans for the future. It is possible that one of your chief concerns will be Christmas, which is only a month away. When it comes to domestic chores, do your best to be inventive and to change the order in which you do things.

26 MONDAY   *Moon Age Day 17   Moon Sign Gemini*

You can now change the way you communicate with others. It may be that you are being much more selective in the people you approach, and you might also be happy to leave alone those who regularly cause problems for you. Aquarius could be just a little more selfish than usual right now.

27 TUESDAY   *Moon Age Day 18   Moon Sign Cancer*

Trends offer you a relaxing and interesting sort of day but also a time during which you can think deeply about an issue that has been on your mind for some time. If you remain relaxed you can now deal with situations better and can find answers that have eluded you for a few weeks or even months.

28 WEDNESDAY   *Moon Age Day 19   Moon Sign Cancer*

Whenever it proves to be possible you need to widen your horizons. Don't just look at the possible, but seek to stretch yourself whenever you can. The tendency to feel bored by life is still hovering around and you need to do everything you can to counteract this trend. Seeking out interesting people and new situations can work wonders.

29 THURSDAY   *Moon Age Day 20   Moon Sign Leo*

The Moon is now in Leo and that means you are under the influence of the lunar low. With some strong supporting planetary influences you may hardly notice the less positive aspects of this time, though a quieter interlude is possible, offering you a chance to spend more hours on your own than would usually be the case.

30 FRIDAY

Moon Age Day 21   Moon Sign Leo

Even if you decide to slow down the current pace of events, that doesn't mean you have to stop altogether. What is really necessary is more concentration on specific matters, whilst you leave others to sort out routine jobs. Support from family members can prove to be especially useful around this time.

December
2007

1 SATURDAY
Moon Age Day 22   Moon Sign Virgo

The start of December brings situations that could take you by surprise. Most of these are likely to be positive in nature and offer you an opportunity to reap the benefits of efforts you have put in previously. You have what it takes to put the warmest and most endearing qualities of your nature on display this weekend.

2 SUNDAY
Moon Age Day 23   Moon Sign Virgo

Whilst you are definitely on the move again you would be wise to exercise just a little care today. There are new people to meet and exciting situations to address. The only slight fly in the ointment is the way you approach both people and events. Avoid coming on too strong and be as 'cool' as you can.

3 MONDAY
Moon Age Day 24   Moon Sign Virgo

Even if personal relationships are rather downbeat at present, you need to take your joys where you can find them. Today that means friendship and the support that particular individuals are offering. In a practical sense it would be best not to take anything for granted, especially at work.

4 TUESDAY
Moon Age Day 25   Moon Sign Libra

Rather than rushing ahead like some people today, being careful is what counts for you. Whilst others have to repeat procedures time and again, you can get them right first time round. Focusing on the small details right now should give you what you need to get in front of the pack.

5 WEDNESDAY
Moon Age Day 26   Moon Sign Libra

Wednesday should offer a period of swifter progress. If you put on a spurt you can steal a march on someone who has been beating you to the punch, though without upsetting them too much. What matters at present is convincing yourself that you are as capable as you believe yourself to be when you are at your most confident.

6 THURSDAY
Moon Age Day 27   Moon Sign Scorpio

Be prepared to seek out the company of interesting and witty people right now and to get ahead in ways you haven't been expecting. For all this you can thank a host of small planetary influences, which when working together should help you to focus on an exciting and uncluttered horizon.

7 FRIDAY
Moon Age Day 28   Moon Sign Scorpio

There are signs that a person higher up the career ladder than you are can steer you in the right direction, if you are only willing to listen to what they say. Reliance on friends can be stronger now and new friendships could be formed around this period. At least part of your mind may now be focused on the Christmas period.

8 SATURDAY
Moon Age Day 29   Moon Sign Scorpio

The more you put yourself about at the moment, the greater should be your sense of achievement. Although you might not be able to take the starring role in everything, you are unlikely to be moved too much by this fact. By the evening you can afford to have your sights set on interesting social possibilities.

9 SUNDAY
Moon Age Day 0   Moon Sign Sagittarius

Even if you are in the mood for Christmas shopping today, you would be wise to avoid making spur of the moment purchases and instead, save your money for another day. Why not ask friends for help and advice? Make certain you listen carefully to what they are saying.

10 MONDAY   *Moon Age Day 1   Moon Sign Sagittarius*

Rather than being too tied down with the realities of work today, you have scope to have fun, and can find people who are willing to help you do so. Stay away from negative people, or the sort of individuals who are backbiting and cruel. The closer you are to the people you are dealing with personally, the better you should feel.

11 TUESDAY   *Moon Age Day 2   Moon Sign Capricorn*

Taking care of minor details will probably occupy some of your time today, but you should have a broader and more expansive interest in life too. This shows itself in a number of different ways, but as the day wears on you could notice that you are slightly quieter than has been the case for quite a few days.

12 WEDNESDAY   *Moon Age Day 3   Moon Sign Capricorn*

A day to take some time out to think things through. If you keep your mind uncluttered with details, you should be able to see clearly through to the heart of most situations. It's worth reassuring those with whom you live that you have been thinking about the festive season and that many of the necessary details are sorted.

13 THURSDAY   *Moon Age Day 4   Moon Sign Capricorn*

Personalities tend to enter your life at the moment, or at least that is how it seems. The truth of the matter may be that you are not shining quite so brightly yourself at present and so tend to notice the positive points of others more. The Moon in your solar twelfth house encourages you to be quite contemplative.

14 FRIDAY   *Moon Age Day 5   Moon Sign Aquarius*

The most important physical peak of the month comes along now, thanks to the lunar high. For a couple of days you should be feeling extremely fit and willing to take on just about any task that comes your way. Keep as distant as you can from tedious jobs at the moment, sticking instead to what gives you pleasure.

15 SATURDAY   *Moon Age Day 6   Moon Sign Aquarius*

The lunar high is still around and there are gains to be made, even in unexpected directions. Money matters ought to be easier and you can make the most of extra energy. Now you really can chance your arm, which is pretty much in line with the Aquarian nature when working at its best.

16 SUNDAY   *Moon Age Day 7   Moon Sign Pisces*

Your strength lies in keeping life light and bright and not taking yourself or anyone else more seriously than you have to. The sort of people with whom you choose to mix today need to be individuals who have a good sense of humour and who are willing to make some of the running. You can take delight in interesting conversations.

17 MONDAY   *Moon Age Day 8   Moon Sign Pisces*

Some fairly interesting news may be available now, and this allows you to address your own needs and wishes. Getting on with the task in hand is paramount, but is occasionally difficult with so many distractions coming in from all quarters. You already have one eye on the needs of Christmas.

18 TUESDAY   *Moon Age Day 9   Moon Sign Aries*

Don't be afraid to take on novel interests at this time and be willing to look at new ways of doing things. There is some good advice around at present, as long as you are willing to look at it with an open mind. Creative potential remains essentially good, so now might be a good time to put up the tree and the decorations.

19 WEDNESDAY   *Moon Age Day 10   Moon Sign Aries*

Stronger than normal ego tendencies are possible under present trends. You might be taking on rather too much just now and a little fresh air would do you good. You need some space to think things through and to put the brakes on your present tendency to lord it slightly over others. This isn't usual for Aquarius.

20 THURSDAY   *Moon Age Day 11   Moon Sign Taurus*

Even if the sort of excitement you seem to be looking for at the moment is absent, you can make it for yourself if you are willing to put in that extra bit of effort. You can persuade relatives and friends to join in and can dream up some novel ways to entertain both them and yourself.

21 FRIDAY   *Moon Age Day 12   Moon Sign Taurus*

Your powers of attraction are strong right now, and that can prove to be very useful. The bearing you have on the thinking processes of those around you may be quite surprising, and could lead you to taking the odd risk when dealing with your partner or sweetheart. In at least one matter you can afford to throw caution to the wind.

22 SATURDAY   *Moon Age Day 13   Moon Sign Gemini*

As a direct contrast to yesterday, personal relationships might not appear to be doing you too much in the way of favours today. As a result you may decide to concentrate more on friends than on your partner or family members. A word of caution – with Christmas so close this is no time to be taking on too much in terms of new projects.

23 SUNDAY   *Moon Age Day 14   Moon Sign Gemini*

This would be a good day for asking questions and for gathering new information about life and the part you play in it. Be careful with last-minute shopping. It's possible that you could be fooled into thinking that you are getting a bargain, when you know in your heart that you are being conned.

24 MONDAY   *Moon Age Day 15   Moon Sign Cancer*

There are signs that getting stuck with mundane routines won't appeal to you very much at all now. On the contrary you are more likely to be busy in a practical sense and away from home for at least some of the time. If people are relying heavily on you, the pressure you are under might begin to show at some stage.

25 TUESDAY
Moon Age Day 16   Moon Sign Cancer

You can make Christmas Day a huge hoot, though you may begin to flag later in the day. If there is a journey to be made, why not get it out of the way early and then find time to sit down and put your feet up? What shows most clearly throughout the whole day is how well your sense of humour goes down with those around you.

26 WEDNESDAY
Moon Age Day 17   Moon Sign Leo

Boxing Day may well bring a lessening of the amount of energy at your disposal. This really is the sort of day when you ought to be thinking about simple pleasures and good company. Being an Aquarian you are probably on the go for most of the time, so there is nothing wrong at all with taking a break.

27 THURSDAY
Moon Age Day 18   Moon Sign Leo

The Moon is still in Leo and that means the lunar low can have a bearing on your attitudes and actions. As New Year approaches you can get yourself right back on form, but for the moment you can make the most of this opportunity to watch and wait. Anything with an artistic association has potential to please you today.

28 FRIDAY
Moon Age Day 19   Moon Sign Leo

Although you begin today with the Moon in Leo, by the afternoon the planetary situation will have changed markedly. You might begin to wonder why you have been so lethargic and will rapidly make sure you become the life and soul of any party that is in the offing. A day to show real support for any relative or friend who is in need.

29 SATURDAY
Moon Age Day 20   Moon Sign Virgo

This is a day when you should be prepared to let everyone know exactly who you are. Once you have decided on a particular course of action at present, you can afford to stick with it to the bitter end. New Year resolutions should already be on your mind, and you might even be putting some of them into action early.

30 SUNDAY   *Moon Age Day 21   Moon Sign Virgo*

Today is an excellent time for social get-togethers of almost any sort. If you are willing to mix business with pleasure you can help yourself no end and could even end up gaining in ways that are really surprising. Your naturally friendly ways are fully on display and you can use them to get you some special favours.

31 MONDAY   *Moon Age Day 22   Moon Sign Libra*

There are some great things happening on the social horizon and you ought to be in a good position to gain from them today. Any slight frustration that the holidays are preventing you from getting ahead in more practical ways should soon be forgotten once you decide to immerse yourself in the New Year celebrations.

AQUARIUS:
2008 DIARY PAGES

AQUARIUS:
2008 IN BRIEF

As is usually the case for Aquarius, you look towards a new year with great optimism and a degree of excitement. January and February should not let you down because both months are likely to be dynamic and enterprising. Don't be fooled into thinking that other people know better than you do because chances are they don't. Take the line of least resistance when dealing with romantic matters.

March and April are likely to offer you more in the way of personal happiness. Not that you are ever really stuck for long in any situation, but disagreements may have been present and you can now put these right. More money could be on the way in April, which is also an excellent time to go travelling and to make more of yourself in competitive situations.

It is likely that the early summer months will turn out to be some of the best for you in an all-round sense. This is partly because Lady Luck is favouring your efforts to a greater extent but it is also true that May and June bring you to a much firmer understanding of what you actually want from your life. You remain quite enigmatic from the perspective of others and will need to explain yourself frequently. All the same it is your mystery that makes you so attractive to the world.

July and August are the hottest months in more ways than one as far as Aquarius is concerned. It is at this time that personal relationships are heating up no end and when romance is probably the most important factor in your life as a whole. There may be a renewed commitment to an old task and also a chance for you to get in touch with people you haven't seen for ages. Almost everyone you know seems to be working for your betterment during this interlude.

You should welcome the autumn with open arms because it will increase your ability to get to new places and to see things that have only been a dream to you previously. Don't be too concerned at this time with practical achievements or financial success because these follow naturally if you are taking the right path. September and October bring great vigour and an enhanced love for anything unusual.

November and December might at first sight seem the least helpful to you because a number of obstacles are being put in your path. However, it is with the resolution of these that you come to a better understanding of yourself and of life. The Christmas period should be packed with possibilities and may not turn out the way you expected. Finish the year with a flourish and in possession of your usual optimism about the future.

January 2008

1 TUESDAY
Moon Age Day 23   Moon Sign Libra

The first day of the year could end up being a good deal more active than you might have expected. There is plenty of energy on offer, and you would be wise to direct it immediately into getting on well during the coming year. Aquarius is filled with ideas, not that there is anything remotely strange about that.

2 WEDNESDAY
Moon Age Day 24   Moon Sign Libra

Be careful if you notice one or two contentious issues beginning to surface around this time. It might be best to avoid getting involved in anything controversial, and to remain as honest as possible with yourself and everyone else. If you stay squeaky clean and totally communicative, nobody can find fault with you.

3 THURSDAY
Moon Age Day 25   Moon Sign Scorpio

Life could turn out to be slightly more complicated than you might wish, though probably through no real fault of your own. Using a combination of common sense and intuition you can circumnavigate a few potential pitfalls but it has to be said that you may not exactly be at your luckiest between now and the weekend.

4 FRIDAY
Moon Age Day 26   Moon Sign Scorpio

One safe harbour at the moment could well be personal attachments, which you can get working extremely well and can bring you a good deal of contentment. That's probably more than can be said for practical or professional matters, a few of which may be going askew. Why not seek out the good advice of friends?

5 SATURDAY · *Moon Age Day 27 Moon Sign Sagittarius*

Your ability to attract new admirers is highlighted at the moment. The position of Venus in your solar chart encourages you to make yourself appealing to possible suitors. That's fine unless you are already attached – in which case you might have to make a few declarations to avoid jealousy becoming an issue.

6 SUNDAY · *Moon Age Day 28 Moon Sign Sagittarius*

Emotions can be quite close to the surface today and that could well make you a little more reactive and maybe slightly tetchy on occasions. At least if you are aware of these possibilities you can deal with them quickly and so avoid any fall-outs. A day to seek out positive news of family members.

7 MONDAY · *Moon Age Day 29 Moon Sign Sagittarius*

A new working week dawns, offering you a chance to get yourself noticed. With a gradual rise in your level of luck and greater incentives coming along all the time it could seem as if life itself is lending you a hand this week. Even if today makes demands on your time, you have what it takes to deal with these wonderfully.

8 TUESDAY · *Moon Age Day 0 Moon Sign Capricorn*

Be prepared to seek advice and stimulation from those you meet both at work and socially. Even the most insignificant facts can prove to be important at present, so it's worth keeping your ears open. Aquarius isn't averse to a little gossip, and there could be plenty of that about now.

9 WEDNESDAY · *Moon Age Day 1 Moon Sign Capricorn*

You have scope for a slightly quieter day because the Moon is passing through your solar twelfth house on its way back to your own zodiac sign of Aquarius. It's worth finding moments to think and to get things right. What is more you may decide to spend a few hours with your partner and this could prove to be extremely rewarding.

10 THURSDAY   *Moon Age Day 2 Moon Sign Aquarius*

Today the Moon moves into the zodiac sign of Aquarius, bringing that part of the month that is known as the lunar high. You can make the most of a higher level of general good luck and can afford to back your hunches to a greater extent. It's true that there are changes in the offing but nearly all of these are potentially advantageous.

11 FRIDAY   *Moon Age Day 3 Moon Sign Aquarius*

This is one of the best days of the month for putting new plans into operation. Don't hold back when you know in your heart that your ideas are sound and enlist the support of people who can be persuaded to follow your lead. You can feather not only your own nest right now but those of your colleagues and friends too.

12 SATURDAY   *Moon Age Day 4 Moon Sign Pisces*

Even if you know that domestic partners have your best interests at heart this Saturday, the same may not be the case out there in the wider world. Your best approach is to avoid taking on commitments about which you are not entirely certain. A slight delay can't hurt much and will give you time to think.

13 SUNDAY   *Moon Age Day 5 Moon Sign Pisces*

The demands coming in from the outside world could well keep you on your toes just now but you can still find a few moments for the more intimate aspects of your life. Some Aquarians might now begin to feel the need to make significant changes in or around the home, but there may be very little time to act upon such desires today.

14 MONDAY   *Moon Age Day 6 Moon Sign Pisces*

You continue to be very busy, either out there in the world or at the very least inside your head. The Aquarian mind is rarely still for long, and this assists you to follow up on hunches that began late last week. If people don't respond in the way you expect, you have the persuasive powers to bring them round.

15 TUESDAY   *Moon Age Day 7 Moon Sign Aries*

Monetary issues are well accented, and you can now consider taking on those commitments that you shied away from at the weekend. You have scope to seek out a bargain if you go shopping today and your general level of good luck seems to be positively maintained throughout much of this week.

16 WEDNESDAY   *Moon Age Day 8 Moon Sign Aries*

Although it would be very sensible to think before you act today there could be certain occasions when there simply isn't time. That's where your instincts come in, and these should be honed to perfection at the present time. Few people could hope to get ahead of you in the career stakes and you can shine like a star when in social settings.

17 THURSDAY   *Moon Age Day 9 Moon Sign Taurus*

A day to remain generally easy-going and very much in tune with your financial goals. This is a good time for beginning new investments or changing a few existing ones, and your whole mind can be incredibly expansive and outgoing. You show a strong mixture between the need for financial security and the desire to spread your wings.

18 FRIDAY   *Moon Age Day 10 Moon Sign Taurus*

To say that you can get yourself noticed at present is an understatement. Aquarius can be one of the most chatty and likeable signs of the zodiac and there is certainly no doubt about that fact just now. Make the most of these positive trends by staying in good company. There is no point in hiding your light under a bushel today.

19 SATURDAY   *Moon Age Day 11 Moon Sign Gemini*

The weekend should see you maintaining the good times, not least if you make sure you seize the moment. You could also be quite creative at this time and can make your personal surroundings as comfortable and beautiful as possible. Friends might be difficult early in the day but should settle later.

20 SUNDAY
Moon Age Day 12 Moon Sign Gemini

Getting your ideas across should be the easiest part of your life whilst Venus keeps its present position in your solar chart. Whether you are dealing with practical matters or love, you have what it takes to explain yourself in ways that others both understand and relish. Aquarius does need adulation and has potential to attract it now.

21 MONDAY
Moon Age Day 13 Moon Sign Cancer

Be prepared to fire up your ambitions and step forward and be counted when it comes to new responsibilities. Even if not everyone is totally on your side today, a little competition does you no real harm at all and on the contrary it encourages you to hone your intellect. Don't deal in standard responses today but try something new.

22 TUESDAY
Moon Age Day 14 Moon Sign Cancer

Today can be positive as far as money is concerned, and you needn't be at all fazed by having to change any horse in midstream. On the contrary, change is very important to you and although there is a potentially quieter spell on the way tomorrow, the general pattern of your life is upward and onward well into the future.

23 WEDNESDAY
Moon Age Day 15 Moon Sign Leo

The Moon enters Leo, which is your opposite zodiac sign. This brings a two-day period that crops up each month and which is known as the lunar low. Extra pressure is a possibility, whilst getting ahead today could seem like walking through treacle. It might be best to leave some of the real work to others.

24 THURSDAY
Moon Age Day 16 Moon Sign Leo

Rather than expecting everything to go exactly as you had planned, be willing to stand back and think again if you know in your heart it is necessary to do so. There are reversals today, but none of these should prove to be either serious or long-lasting. Instead of trying to fight against the tide, why not take some time out to wallow in the shallows?

25 FRIDAY
Moon Age Day 17 Moon Sign Virgo

Trends suggest slight problems in social relationships. You may find it difficult to achieve any sort of compromise where you are at odds with others. There is a way round any situation and it is simply a matter of thinking harder. It's worth removing yourself from conflict before arguments arise.

26 SATURDAY
Moon Age Day 18 Moon Sign Virgo

The focus is on your ambitions at present, and you have what it takes to get what you want from life and people. That doesn't mean you should bulldoze your ideas through, and it is vitally important today that you explain yourself carefully and also listen to points of view that might be very different from yours.

27 SUNDAY
Moon Age Day 19 Moon Sign Libra

When it comes to money matters you would be wise to stay on the ball. You shouldn't relinquish control of your own money, nor trust anyone except an intimate to deal with cash on your behalf. All in all you seem to be quite materialistic at this stage of the month, but you do need to avoid becoming boring about the whole issue!

28 MONDAY
Moon Age Day 20 Moon Sign Libra

Though optimism and positive thinking are important at the present time, you can afford to rest on occasions and allow some situations to sort themselves out. Routines can be fairly comfortable for now and it would be very easy to settle back and allow colleagues to take most of the strain – but it won't happen, will it?

29 TUESDAY ☿
Moon Age Day 21 Moon Sign Libra

This may not be the most progressive day of the month, but you can make sure it is fairly happy, and your level of contentment in a personal sense can be going off the scale. You may feel less inclined to push the bounds of the possible as far as your professional life is concerned, and may decide to seek more in the way of affection.

30 WEDNESDAY ☿ *Moon Age Day 22 Moon Sign Scorpio*

When it comes to making agreements with others you need to be rather careful at the moment because you could get yourself into situations in which you would rather not be involved. Look out for gifts coming your way later in the day – even if these are not wrapped in paper and tied with ribbons they should be very welcome.

31 THURSDAY ☿ *Moon Age Day 23 Moon Sign Scorpio*

Although there may be more responsibilities about between now and the weekend, you needn't let these trouble you too much. Make compromises today and you will find that the level of help and support you can attract from others is much greater than you might expect. Your social popularity is potentially high.

♒ February 2008

1 FRIDAY
☿ *Moon Age Day 24 Moon Sign Sagittarius*

It's not worth arguing over details today because it is the broader spectrum of life that matters the most. If you go with the flow instead of trying to tinker with things, you can achieve progress. A positive response to others is the best way to create happiness.

2 SATURDAY
☿ *Moon Age Day 25 Moon Sign Sagittarius*

If you have new information at your disposal you need to use it for all you are worth. Aquarius is usually in the know and that's because you keep your eyes and ears open. Be careful that friends do not become too demanding because for at least part of this weekend you need to do what exclusively pleases you.

3 SUNDAY
☿ *Moon Age Day 26 Moon Sign Sagittarius*

Working with people you like can be extremely satisfying today and you may not be keen to push yourself harder than proves to be necessary. The weather outside might not be all that startling, but a little fresh air and a change of scenery would do you the world of good. All work and no play can make Aquarius dull and listless.

4 MONDAY
☿ *Moon Age Day 27 Moon Sign Capricorn*

The present position of Mercury allows you to enhance your creative thinking. Some of your ideas are distinctly original – though of course there is nothing especially unusual about that for Aquarius. Most important of all is your ability to get to almost any winning post without having to run the circuit.

5 TUESDAY   ☿ *Moon Age Day 28 Moon Sign Capricorn*

Although there might be some tensions in personal relationships, in the main you should be able to get on well with almost everyone. Today offers an opportunity to use an air of mystery to your distinct advantage. There are gains to be made from keeping some people guessing.

6 WEDNESDAY   ☿ *Moon Age Day 0 Moon Sign Aquarius*

The lunar high is a time for keeping up your diversity of interests and not being so centred on one task that you fail to see how well other things are turning out. It's early in the year yet but you may decide that this would still be a good time to take a trip. Winter doesn't really bother you at all, so why not get out there and have fun?

7 THURSDAY   ☿ *Moon Age Day 1 Moon Sign Aquarius*

What really counts at the moment is variety, which as they say is the spice of life. That's certainly true for you, and together with your unconventional way of doing things you can attract a good deal of attention from colleagues and friends. Be prepared to help a reluctant family member out of a rut.

8 FRIDAY   ☿ *Moon Age Day 2 Moon Sign Aquarius*

You can look at matters today in a very different way and could well be happiest when you are left to your own devices to sort things out. The only slight fly in the ointment at the moment comes if you sense interference taking place. If there is one thing that works for you at the moment it is a certain degree of privacy.

9 SATURDAY   ☿ *Moon Age Day 3 Moon Sign Pisces*

Even if domestic and family matters are demanding most of your attention today, there should still be moments during which you can do whatever takes your fancy. You might be in the market for a spot of shopping and if so you have scope to find a bargain or two. You can afford to spend some quality time later with your partner.

10 SUNDAY ☿ *Moon Age Day 4 Moon Sign Pisces*

It looks as though some Aquarians could be thrust straight into the limelight, and although this needn't bother you there is a chance you will be unprepared for what is coming. From a social point of view you should be happy to lead the way, even if you are expected to do something you have never undertaken before.

11 MONDAY ☿ *Moon Age Day 5 Moon Sign Aries*

Today is favourable for all business transactions and for professional partnerships. As is often the case for Aquarius you have that certain knack for mixing business with pleasure, and you can use it to seek out some very interesting individuals around this time. Confronting an issue from the past is also possible sometime today.

12 TUESDAY ☿ *Moon Age Day 6 Moon Sign Aries*

Whilst you might be filled with confidence and happy to have a go at almost anything, the same may not be true for colleagues or some friends. You may spend so much time convincing others to take the plunge that you never actually get wet at all. If you really want to make progress, you might decide to go it alone today.

13 WEDNESDAY ☿ *Moon Age Day 7 Moon Sign Taurus*

Diversity is now the key to real happiness – not that this is very unusual for you. What might bore you today would be to get stuck in a rut and to have little chance of making the progress in life that you sense is possible around now. For this reason you should avoid mixing with people who move at the pace of a tortoise.

14 THURSDAY ☿ *Moon Age Day 8 Moon Sign Taurus*

It might be better to give way today rather than to argue about issues that really are not significant. Don't overestimate your own importance or you may end up being somewhat disappointed. On the other hand, if you show a high degree of modesty you have a chance to attract compliments – which is very pleasant.

15 FRIDAY ☿ *Moon Age Day 9 Moon Sign Gemini*

An ideal time to seek out people who have a happy-go-lucky attitude and who are willing to bend with the wind. Once again you could find difficulties if you allow yourself to be surrounded by pessimists. Your own attitude to life at the moment is a little like throwing stones in ponds to see how big the splashes are.

16 SATURDAY ☿ *Moon Age Day 10 Moon Sign Gemini*

Co-operation is definitely to be recommended, though maybe more at home than in any professional arena. You may not have noticed but the weekend has arrived and that should mean more time to do what pleases you. You can afford to remain generally happy with your lot, even if not everyone around you is exactly overflowing with joy.

17 SUNDAY ☿ *Moon Age Day 11 Moon Sign Cancer*

If you decide that a little restructuring of your personal life is necessary at the moment, your best approach is to move forward carefully and don't upset others by speaking too rashly or out of turn. Older family members may have the right words of wisdom to keep you on course, so why not listen to what they have to say?

18 MONDAY ☿ *Moon Age Day 12 Moon Sign Cancer*

A slightly slower start to the week will at least give you time to think before you act and that can be quite important just now. The lunar low is approaching so there may not be quite the level of progress for the next few days that you have anticipated or wished for. Alternative ways of doing things should be explored.

19 TUESDAY ☿ *Moon Age Day 13 Moon Sign Leo*

The Moon now in the zodiac sign of Leo encourages you to be more reserved, less inclined to speak your mind and probably not half so sure of yourself as has been the case recently. Others may think you are sulking about something, so it's important to at least appear cheerful, even if you have things on your mind.

20 WEDNESDAY — Moon Age Day 14 Moon Sign Leo

The introspective phase continues, and you may choose your own company more than that of other people. From your point of view this is just fine but the same people whom you urged onward a few days ago are now waiting for you to catch up. For the moment you may be happy to saunter along.

21 THURSDAY — Moon Age Day 15 Moon Sign Leo

As today wears on you should gradually be able to find your feet more and get yourself out there in the social mainstream. Trends support a careful approach to money, and to any situations with financial complications. It would be better to keep everything as simple as possible now.

22 FRIDAY — Moon Age Day 16 Moon Sign Virgo

You can make the most of some strong progressive influences today, not least those that come from people you have helped in the recent past. Now it's their turn to lend you a hand, even if you are not exactly sure you need it. In all social situations you can show yourself to be cultured, refined and able to carry yourself well.

23 SATURDAY — Moon Age Day 17 Moon Sign Virgo

Be careful today because you might just be a little too assertive for your own good. It's great to be confident and to show other people that you are, but you could be taking the wind out of someone's sails without realising. It's worth being especially considerate of the feelings of family members and good friends.

24 SUNDAY — Moon Age Day 18 Moon Sign Libra

You have a great talent at the moment for creating harmony. This has little to do with your singing prowess in any local karaoke but is more closely related to your abilities to bring other people closer together. You have what it takes to play the honest broker in more ways than one, and can make friendships even deeper.

25 MONDAY
Moon Age Day 19 Moon Sign Libra

Personal matters are potentially more rewarding today than professional or practical ones. Trends support spending time with your partner, or pursuing a new relationship if you are unattached. Even if not everyone loves you today, the most important people should do.

26 TUESDAY
Moon Age Day 20 Moon Sign Scorpio

Look out for tension in some relationships. Although this may not be caused by you, there is still a chance that you will be on the receiving end. You need to be as understanding as proves to be possible, whilst remaining fairly firm about your own opinions. As long as you are honest with yourself and others, you can make sure everything is fine.

27 WEDNESDAY
Moon Age Day 21 Moon Sign Scorpio

It might seem warm and comfortable in your own little world today but that's not where things are likely to happen. There's just a chance you are withdrawing because there is something to be done that you don't relish. If this is the case, your best approach is to get it out of the way as soon as you can, leaving you free to do more enjoyable things.

28 THURSDAY
Moon Age Day 22 Moon Sign Scorpio

Even if this isn't the luckiest day of the month so far, it can have its own particular rewards. These are more likely to be of a personal nature, and you might even be able to attract an admirer you never previously suspected. Try not to create a situation of envy or jealousy.

29 FRIDAY
Moon Age Day 23 Moon Sign Sagittarius

Personal issues remain to fore, indicating a more introspective Aquarius than has been the case so far this year. Even if you don't show yourself as being bold or adventurous today, you can at least pretend when you know there is a degree of expectation coming from the direction of others.

March

2008

1 SATURDAY
Moon Age Day 24 Moon Sign Sagittarius

Now you have what it takes to persuade others to see things in the way you do. All of a sudden it should be easier to get your point of view across, and to make your mark outside your own private little world. Your attitude to many matters can be both unconventional and distinctly original – which is Aquarian!

2 SUNDAY
Moon Age Day 25 Moon Sign Capricorn

You have the ability to be mentally sharp and spot on with most of your assumptions. This is a Sunday that can offer much in the way of personal freedom, and on which you needn't feel restricted in any way, shape or form. In sporting endeavours you can afford to go for gold – though it's the taking part that counts.

3 MONDAY
Moon Age Day 26 Moon Sign Capricorn

You can once again retreat into your own world more than usual. This time the culprit is a twelfth-house Moon, which encourages you to be more introspective and less gregarious. This is a time of preparation, or at least it should be. By Wednesday you can make sure things look very different.

4 TUESDAY
Moon Age Day 27 Moon Sign Capricorn

Even if you approach life in a slower and steadier way than has been generally the case for the last few weeks, at least you can get things right first time and that could prove to be very important. New objectives are in view and some of these are worth thinking about deeply before you commit yourself. For once Aquarius can be very cautious.

5 WEDNESDAY   *Moon Age Day 28 Moon Sign Aquarius*

At last the Moon returns to your zodiac sign, bringing the lunar high and supporting a more outgoing and courageous approach. Almost nothing is beyond you now, and competitors had better watch out. On a personal level you have what it takes to be joyful, poetic and filled with charm. Who could fail to love you at the moment?

6 THURSDAY   *Moon Age Day 29 Moon Sign Aquarius*

Lady Luck is on your side and that allows you to be slightly less cautious about taking the odd chance. This doesn't mean putting your shirt on the next horse running, though you can make the most of a strong and powerful intuition. Be prepared to strike whilst the iron is hot, and to encourage others to do so.

7 FRIDAY   *Moon Age Day 0 Moon Sign Pisces*

It might be necessary to apply the brakes a little if you sense that some aspects of your life are getting slightly out of control. In particular you need to be more careful when it comes to personal attachments. There is just a small chance that your natural kindness is being misconstrued, and that could lead to trouble later.

8 SATURDAY   *Moon Age Day 1 Moon Sign Pisces*

The weekend works best if you are warm, attentive and especially kind to people who are less well off than you are. This charitable side to your nature will be well emphasised throughout much of March, assisting you to do what you can to make the world a better place. Happiness can be found in unexpected places today.

9 SUNDAY   *Moon Age Day 2 Moon Sign Aries*

Places of luxury and enjoyment could well appeal to you greatly around now and this Sunday marks an interlude when there is less emphasis on practical matters and more on spoiling yourself in some way. Why not get together with friends to do something quite exciting and maybe just slightly risqué?

10 MONDAY   *Moon Age Day 3 Moon Sign Aries*

Today is excellent for everyday communications and especially for getting your message across at work. You can make sure that just about everyone you know benefits from having you around today and that they realise the fact. If there is one thing that is really important to Aquarius it is being appreciated.

11 TUESDAY   *Moon Age Day 4 Moon Sign Taurus*

Even if things are slightly sluggish professionally, in a more personal sense they are well accented for most Aquarians. You know how to hand out the compliments and these should be very well received right now. Confidence to do the right thing remains essentially high, but beware self-doubt.

12 WEDNESDAY   *Moon Age Day 5 Moon Sign Taurus*

Slight tensions within personal relationships are best sorted out as soon as possible. These can detract from your general progress in life at a time when you really do need all your concentration. It would be best today to do one thing at once, because the present position of the planet Mars doesn't encourage you to multi-task.

13 THURSDAY   *Moon Age Day 6 Moon Sign Gemini*

Today works best if you don't emphasise the really impulsive side of your nature. A slightly low-key approach to most situations is what is presently called for. If there are problems somewhere within the family, don't be afraid to be on hand to sort them out almost immediately.

14 FRIDAY   *Moon Age Day 7 Moon Sign Gemini*

Remaining objective and in the main sensible, you have what it takes to get ahead steadily, but is that enough? It's a fact that Aquarians soon get bored unless something special is on the horizon. Maybe the time is right to start thinking about old things in new ways, not to mention making more of a physical effort.

15 SATURDAY
Moon Age Day 8 Moon Sign Cancer

The weekend offers better trends, plus a great ability to be in the right place at the best possible time. Your strength lies in getting on well with most people, so if anyone really awkward does come along you can sidestep them altogether. In the main the focus is on spending time with those who are special to you.

16 SUNDAY
Moon Age Day 9 Moon Sign Cancer

You needn't let slightly wacky things that other people do upset you in the least. After all, you come from what can be the craziest zodiac sign of them all. You can show yourself to be original, inspirational, unusual and sometimes even downright odd. All of this certainly helps you to get yourself noticed and to play to the crowd.

17 MONDAY
Moon Age Day 10 Moon Sign Cancer

With the start of a new working week comes the chance to do something very, very different. That's fine, but do bear in mind that with the lunar low coming along tomorrow you may well be stopped in your tracks. It might be best to plan ahead to Thursday, whilst keeping a fairly conservative approach in the meantime.

18 TUESDAY
Moon Age Day 11 Moon Sign Leo

Be prepared to avoid important decisions for the moment, or at least sidestep them until later. You don't have what it takes to impress people to the same extent as during the last few days, and may not want to in any case. It isn't that you are miserable but you may well be happiest with your own company for now.

19 WEDNESDAY
Moon Age Day 12 Moon Sign Leo

Trying to remain objective can be quite hard under present trends. Even if part of you longs to break free and to show your genuine originality, other facets of your nature are keener to hold back. If there is a problem today it could be that life contains very few blacks and whites and is mostly composed of different shades of grey.

20 THURSDAY
Moon Age Day 13 Moon Sign Virgo

You can now be back in the swing, almost from the moment you get out of bed. What a difference a day makes, especially to an Air sign such as yours. Now you really can put your new plans into action, and have what it takes to get other people to lend a hand. Romance looks especially good for today and tomorrow.

21 FRIDAY
Moon Age Day 14 Moon Sign Virgo

Domestic harmony seems fairly easy to achieve, not just because of your state of mind but also on account of how you deal with relatives, some of whom may be going to special lengths to please you. At work you need to be careful not to be set in your ways. New responsibilities beckon and you can grab them with both hands.

22 SATURDAY
Moon Age Day 15 Moon Sign Libra

Where personal involvements are concerned there is just a small chance of some tension building up today. If there is something you have on your mind it would be better to speak out, albeit tactfully, because you won't gain anything by remaining silent. Friends may tax your patience too but not for long at a time.

23 SUNDAY
Moon Age Day 16 Moon Sign Libra

Today marks a positive interlude during which you have scope to sit back and look at situations from the past. It isn't that you are being overly nostalgic – more that you realise that you can learn something from a situation that is now finished. You may well decide to handle similar matters in a very different way henceforth.

24 MONDAY
Moon Age Day 17 Moon Sign Libra

There is little time today during which to stand and stare. Unlike yesterday, the general pressures of the day are potentially demanding, and it might seem as though you do nothing but work all day long. There are moments later that you can call your own but you need to be in the right frame of mind to appreciate them fully.

25 TUESDAY
Moon Age Day 18 Moon Sign Scorpio

Venus remains in your solar third house so there isn't much doubt about your ability to verbalise the way you feel romantically. You can show your silver-tongued eloquence in other ways too, especially when you are in social settings. Now is the time to prove to others that they benefit from having you around.

26 WEDNESDAY
Moon Age Day 19 Moon Sign Scorpio

The middle of the week may turn out to be the best time from a financial point of view. Not only are you able to deal well with existing circumstances, but you also have good ideas about how you can improve things in the weeks and months ahead. It's worth sharing your inspirations with others because there are important partnerships to be formed.

27 THURSDAY
Moon Age Day 20 Moon Sign Sagittarius

Today can be enjoyable at home but also continues to be a fairly positive period as far as work is concerned. Mixing business with pleasure shouldn't be hard but maybe you should be giving more of your off time to family members. The time is right to impress your partner and stay in their good books.

28 FRIDAY
Moon Age Day 21 Moon Sign Sagittarius

Trends suggest that trivial irritations are possible, so avoiding them would be wise. That's fine as far as it goes, but unless you look at things carefully you might easily get into the odd scrape. Concentration is called for – but unfortunately so is a great deal of patience.

29 SATURDAY
Moon Age Day 22 Moon Sign Sagittarius

The focus is on spending time with people you know well this weekend. Even if you are very keen to have a good time and to get plenty done, you may not be as adventurous as usual. The odd journey could be on the cards and if this is the case you need to keep your eyes skimmed for something special and unusual.

30 SUNDAY · · · *Moon Age Day 23 Moon Sign Capricorn*

There remains a great duality about your nature for the moment. On the one hand you may feel the need to prove yourself but at the same time a twelfth-house Moon encourages you to take life slowly and steadily. That can make for a stop–start sort of day and one during which getting yourself motivated may be difficult.

31 MONDAY · · · *Moon Age Day 24 Moon Sign Capricorn*

You might decide to opt for a quieter sort of Monday, and one on which you will be left alone to do what you want. However, this frame of mind is unlikely to last long because the Moon is racing towards your zodiac sign of Aquarius, where it will be stationed before the end of the day. That could help you to make the evening interesting!

April

2008

1 TUESDAY
Moon Age Day 25 Moon Sign Aquarius

Now you can really get back on form and leave the hesitations of the last couple completely behind. The world shows itself in amazing technicolor and you can't get enough of all that is on offer. In particular the lunar high assists with speaking in public settings and undertaking almost any journey.

2 WEDNESDAY
Moon Age Day 26 Moon Sign Aquarius

The form of good luck that you can tap into today is such that it spills over into just about every facet of your life. Aquarius can now be totally active and enterprising – anxious to get ahead and keen to try almost anything on the road to greater experience. All of this helps you to increase your popularity and gain an audience.

3 THURSDAY
Moon Age Day 27 Moon Sign Pisces

Your home is the ideal setting for social and romantic activities today, even if you are still busy in other ways too. Actually slowing life down might be the hardest thing to do but it is necessary on occasions. You don't want to miss a solid-gold opportunity just because you aren't paying attention.

4 FRIDAY
Moon Age Day 28 Moon Sign Pisces

There are likely to be gains and losses today, but in the main the trends are positive. Routines can be quite tedious, which is why you may choose to ring the changes as much as you can. With the weekend in view you may decide to pep things up socially, and tonight would be as good a time as any.

5 SATURDAY
Moon Age Day 29 Moon Sign Pisces

Rather than being too quick to pick holes in someone else's ideas, why not think about how these can complement your own notions?. Things may not be what they seem, and getting your detective head on could prove to be very informative.

6 SUNDAY
Moon Age Day 0 Moon Sign Aries

With everything to play for and plenty of possibilities available, it would be sensible to keep your eyes peeled today. Don't get too tied down with domestic chores and be willing to take advantage of surprise invitations, even if you have little or no time to think about them. New personalities are part of what today is about.

7 MONDAY
Moon Age Day 1 Moon Sign Aries

This would be a particularly good day on which to express your love for someone, or else to start out on a new relationship. Trends assist you to attract attention and compliments, perhaps from unexpected directions. In a practical sense you have scope to get on with new initiatives too.

8 TUESDAY
Moon Age Day 2 Moon Sign Taurus

Opportunities to get ahead today are more likely to lie in the area of work. New professional possibilities lie around every corner and you can afford to consider taking on alternative or altered responsibilities. April could also bring a greater series of financial incentives, even if you don't exactly recognise these just yet.

9 WEDNESDAY
Moon Age Day 3 Moon Sign Taurus

It's worth turning your focus to joint affairs, especially those that are in some way related to money. At home you might have some difficulty persuading younger family members to toe the line, even if you are paying attention, and possibly even overreacting in some way. The achievements of one close relative could well make you happy.

10 THURSDAY
Moon Age Day 4 Moon Sign Gemini

Your best approach is to make an effort to be transparent to everyone today, rather than your playing your cards very close to your chest. You seem to assume that if you share a particular idea you will lose control of it, but nothing could be further from the truth. Openness is always best for Aquarius.

11 FRIDAY
Moon Age Day 5 Moon Sign Gemini

Intellectual and cultural ideas suit you best right now, and you may also have the chance to be in the company of people you respect and like. You have what it takes to impress all manner of folk but could be especially noticed for your inspirational and even revolutionary approach to work. Nobody can top you for charisma now.

12 SATURDAY
Moon Age Day 6 Moon Sign Cancer

Most romantic relationships are especially well starred for the weekend, even if you find that you are much busier than you might have expected. You should be able to engender a comfortable atmosphere for your lover and still manage to get everything done that seems so important. In the evening you have scope to pep up your social life.

13 SUNDAY
Moon Age Day 7 Moon Sign Cancer

The focus is on feeling happy and secure at the moment. You can use your ego to prevent those bouts of self-doubt that sometimes follow you around. Your strength lies in knowing very well what you want from life and being in the best possible frame of mind to organise situations so you can get it.

14 MONDAY
Moon Age Day 8 Moon Sign Leo

The start of the new working week could be slightly marred by the arrival of the lunar low. If things aren't going exactly as you would wish, you might have to work that much harder to achieve your objectives. What doesn't seem in doubt is your ability to attract help from friends, and it's worth relying on that today.

`15 TUESDAY *Moon Age Day 9 Moon Sign Leo*

Energy levels might still be rather low and you could do worse than to spend some time recharging flagging batteries. That's fine in principle, but in practice you often have masses to do. Don't be too worried about specific tasks, many of which can easily wait for a day or two. What matters most today is contentment and stability.

16 WEDNESDAY *Moon Age Day 10 Moon Sign Virgo*

The Moon moves on into the zodiac sign of Virgo, and together with the position of Mars and Venus offers greater incentives in most spheres of your life. You can afford to feel wonderful today – for no tangible reason. The year is advancing, spring has arrived and there is strong planetary assistance. Don't be afraid to enjoy yourself!

17 THURSDAY *Moon Age Day 11 Moon Sign Virgo*

Now is a good time to capitalise on some of your personal ambitions. Even if the help you give to others is still an important factor in your thinking, you can at least spend more time today feathering your own nest. Make sure you remain organised and practical in your approach, and things should work out just fine.

18 FRIDAY *Moon Age Day 12 Moon Sign Libra*

What matters most today is being in the know, which is why it is vitally important to check all details. Your strength lies in getting to the bottom of things, even if this involves dealing with new technology. Yours is the most technologically motivated sign of them all – you just have to realise the fact.

19 SATURDAY *Moon Age Day 13 Moon Sign Libra*

The busy and interesting interlude continues, though you may well have to struggle just a little in order to get everything you might want. With the weekend comes potential dissatisfaction with domestic matters. This is particularly the case if certain relatives are not doing what you expect.

20 SUNDAY
Moon Age Day 14 Moon Sign Libra

You can afford to maintain a generally happy emotional outlook, and despite any irritations around at home, could be striking out and doing something quite different today. Be prepared to deal with a mixture of responses from friends, some more positive than others.

21 MONDAY
Moon Age Day 15 Moon Sign Scorpio

Why not make an early start today and get stuck into something that has been causing you just a little trouble? Your patience now knows no bounds, and the more complex the task, the happier you can be. Most important of all is the sense of satisfaction when you get to the end of a job. Leading questions are possible later.

22 TUESDAY
Moon Age Day 16 Moon Sign Scorpio

A favourable interlude for any Aquarians who are presently involved in full-time education. This is a great time for all Aquarians to take in new information because the level of concentration is currently enhanced. Theory is better than practice today.

23 WEDNESDAY
Moon Age Day 17 Moon Sign Sagittarius

Life is unlikely to let you down in any major way today, though you may have to work just a little harder if you want to get exactly what you have been hoping for. An ideal day to get in touch with friends you don't see face-to-face very often. Don't be in the least surprised if an old flame begins to burn more brightly in your life during the next few days.

24 THURSDAY
Moon Age Day 18 Moon Sign Sagittarius

Even if you now feel the need to take a far more dominant role in relationships, whether this turns out to be possible under today's planetary trends remains to be seen. Some of your efforts to control others could be doomed to failure, and all things considered you may decide it is better not to try.

25 FRIDAY
Moon Age Day 19 Moon Sign Sagittarius

Some people could say that you are presently looking at life through rose-coloured glasses, but that's part of being an Aquarian. You work best when you are optimistic, and even though not everything goes the way you want you manage to bounce back. Today certainly has ups and downs, but even the downs can have their advantages.

26 SATURDAY
Moon Age Day 20 Moon Sign Capricorn

You have scope to welcome new personalities into your life this weekend and to make use of their presence. Watch out that you don't spend money on things you don't really want, and avoid being taken in by glib talk or false promises. All in all you might choose to keep your purse or wallet firmly closed.

27 SUNDAY
Moon Age Day 21 Moon Sign Capricorn

It is possible that something you have been slightly dreading has now crept up on you whilst you weren't looking. In a way that's a good thing because you won't have much longer to worry about it. Pitch in and get tasks you don't like out of the way as early in the day as you can. By the time this evening arrives you can be on top of things.

28 MONDAY
Moon Age Day 22 Moon Sign Aquarius

The Moon returns to Aquarius and suddenly the world can be your oyster. Now you can put right those little things that have gone wrong in the last few days, and you could also notice that your influence over others is that much greater. There are few limitations placed upon you at the start of this week, so use your imagination!

29 TUESDAY
Moon Age Day 23 Moon Sign Aquarius

This is the best time for putting fresh and innovative ideas to the test, no matter whether they are to do with work or are more personal in nature. The more you socialise this week, the greater should be your sense of enjoyment and fulfilment. If, on the other hand, you do nothing today, you are simply wasting terrific opportunities.

30 WEDNESDAY   *Moon Age Day 24 Moon Sign Aquarius*

It's true taking risks may be required today, but as the saying goes, nothing ventured, nothing gained. As long as you believe in yourself and show the world that you do, you can get others on your side. You can even surprise yourself by taking on some task that would have had you awestruck only a short time ago.

May

2008

1 THURSDAY
Moon Age Day 25 Moon Sign Pisces

The first day of May could be somewhat quieter than has been the case of late, but it still carries opportunities for all Aquarians. You can afford to feel fresh and alive, and should be encouraging others to achieve more. The charitable side of your nature is now much emphasised, but beware of embarrassing others with your kindness.

2 FRIDAY
Moon Age Day 26 Moon Sign Pisces

You may well be rather ego-centred today, and since there is nothing worse than a puffed-up Aquarian, this is a tendency that you would be best off avoiding. Look deep inside yourself and then compare your recent successes with those of other people you know. A sense of proportion is all you need, and then you can move forward modestly.

3 SATURDAY
Moon Age Day 27 Moon Sign Aries

A day to focus most of your energies on making those around you happy. When you are thinking about others you are not concentrating on yourself, and it's a strange fact about your zodiac sign that you are most contented when 'radiating'. Don't be too alarmed if something you have been planning seems to be going slightly awry.

4 SUNDAY
Moon Age Day 28 Moon Sign Aries

Today can be quite fulfilling, though there could be a few frustrations to contend with if you are spending most of the day in or around your home. If you want to avoid these altogether you may decide to get out of the house, perhaps in the company of your partner or a good friend, and ring the changes completely.

5 MONDAY
Moon Age Day 0 Moon Sign Taurus

You might have to cope with a few setbacks at the beginning of this week, though nothing that need have too much of a bearing on your general success. With plenty to play for in the romantic stakes you need to be turning your charisma up to full and wowing your lover at every possible turn.

6 TUESDAY
Moon Age Day 1 Moon Sign Taurus

It looks as though you will be well equipped today to turn all sorts of situations to your advantage. This is predominantly because you are paying attention to what is going on around you and also because your reactions are especially well honed right now. Anyone wishing to beat you to the punch would have to be quick indeed!

7 WEDNESDAY
Moon Age Day 2 Moon Sign Gemini

You may not be quite as patient with certain colleagues or friends as would normally be the case, particularly if they are deliberately doing all they can to upset you. Just when you really seem to be gaining momentum with some task or other, someone throws a spanner in the works. It might better to laugh rather than to grumble.

8 THURSDAY
Moon Age Day 3 Moon Sign Gemini

In serious talks of almost any sort your impact can be immediate and certain, even if part of you doesn't want to take anything at all seriously at the moment. Today is definitely a game of two halves as far as Aquarius is concerned, and it could puzzle people who are around you all day that you can change attitudes so quickly.

9 FRIDAY
Moon Age Day 4 Moon Sign Cancer

Make the best of developments at work and squeeze everything you possibly can out of each advantage that comes your way. By the evening you could be fully committed to social situations and may not want to think about work again for the next couple of days. Why not seek warmth, kindness and inspiration from friends?

10 SATURDAY   *Moon Age Day 5 Moon Sign Cancer*

You can attract help from some unexpected or even highly unlikely directions across the weekend, and make life altogether astonishing. Don't ask too many questions but accept that such periods do come along and that even bizarre coincidences will happen. It's best for now to simply use what is on offer.

11 SUNDAY   *Moon Age Day 6 Moon Sign Leo*

A slightly quieter spell is now on offer as the Moon enters Leo and brings with it the lunar low for the month. After such a hectic time over the last few days you will probably be quite happy to sit back and watch the flowers grow for a while, though there could still be certain emotional issues that have to be discussed today.

12 MONDAY   *Moon Age Day 7 Moon Sign Leo*

Avoid making life difficult for others today with an over-emotional frame of mind. It would be better to spend some time completely on your own than to upset the applecart for everyone else. This interlude doesn't last too long, and can be used to plan your next moves in the professional sphere.

13 TUESDAY   *Moon Age Day 8 Moon Sign Virgo*

There are definite signposts about today and you need to be sure that you don't miss them. All of these can point you in new directions and indicate ways to make more of what you already have. Your creative potential is highlighted at present, helping you to see what changes to make in order to improve your surroundings.

14 WEDNESDAY   *Moon Age Day 9 Moon Sign Virgo*

Even if you don't feel especially energetic for the moment, you can still make steady progress in most areas. What might really annoy you around this time are those people who refuse to take responsibility for their own lives and actions. Maybe Aquarius isn't quite as tolerant right now as it is famous for being as a rule.

15 THURSDAY   *Moon Age Day 10 Moon Sign Virgo*

With a good deal of friendly input on hand you can make quite a lot out of very little. Life resolves itself into two sorts of individuals for you at present. There are those who seem to have your best interests at heart and then there are the individuals who annoy you just by being around. For this reason you need to be extremely selective today.

16 FRIDAY   *Moon Age Day 11 Moon Sign Libra*

Though the period you are now living through has potential to be quite busy from a social point of view, it could be somewhat duller in terms of personal attachments and romance generally. If you want to pep things up you may decide to turn on the charm, buy a surprise present and invite your lover out for an unexpected evening.

17 SATURDAY   *Moon Age Day 12 Moon Sign Libra*

Trends offer you more and more assistance to get your message across to an unsuspecting world as the month wears on. You have masses of energy, a greater than ever desire to make a splash and, maybe most important of all, your sense of humour is back. From a financial point of view it could be hard to save money today.

18 SUNDAY   *Moon Age Day 13 Moon Sign Scorpio*

With Mars now well placed in your solar chart you have scope to be even more assertive and to take the lead amongst your peers. Most of the organisation that goes on around you on this particular Sunday is yours. If you remain sure of yourself at the moment, it is unlikely that anyone would argue with your opinions.

19 MONDAY   *Moon Age Day 14 Moon Sign Scorpio*

A new working week commences for you, offering a great sense of excitement and anticipation. Even awkward or less than pleasurable tasks can now be undertaken with a smile and you could be quite capable of handling half a dozen jobs at the same time. This is Aquarius at its happy and bouncy best.

YOUR DAILY GUIDE TO MAY 2008

20 TUESDAY $\qquad$ *Moon Age Day 15 Moon Sign Scorpio*

There is no doubt about it, you are not a run-of-the-mill sort of person. Aquarians are all a little odd in one way or another but that is what sets them apart and gets them noticed. Your eccentricities are more likely to be in evidence now than at any other time this month, but don't try to suppress them. Glory in being unique!

21 WEDNESDAY *Moon Age Day 16 Moon Sign Sagittarius*

If you feel any stress at all today, you should quickly find ways and means to dissipate it. You would be wise to find a sensible balance between mental and physical pressures. Whether or not you get enough rest remains to be seen, but with so much you want to do that's probably a negative for now.

22 THURSDAY $\qquad$ *Moon Age Day 17 Moon Sign Sagittarius*

The best opportunities for gains right now mean taking the plunge whenever the chance of getting ahead presents itself. That enables you to be right at the front of the queue because you are never tardy when it comes to committing yourself. Few people could keep up your present pace and virtually nobody could beat you off the line.

23 FRIDAY $\qquad$ *Moon Age Day 18 Moon Sign Capricorn*

Trends suggest a slight tendency for you to overspend today and across the weekend, and although this isn't a tragedy, neither is it strictly necessary. The way things are for you in a planetary sense at the moment those possibilities that turn out to be the most enjoyable for you will come totally free of charge, and many are your inspirations.

24 SATURDAY $\qquad$ *Moon Age Day 19 Moon Sign Capricorn*

Getting along with others could now be far easier than proved to be the case a week or so ago, and you might decide to bury the hatchet with someone you haven't been at all friendly towards in the past. The time is right to show your famous tolerance and understanding, and to be at your most accommodating.

25 SUNDAY   *Moon Age Day 20 Moon Sign Capricorn*

This can be a quieter than average Sunday, but if so it comes right out of the blue. It's true that the Moon is now in your solar twelfth house and that this encourages you to be less outgoing, but there are strong supportive planetary positions that say the opposite. The result is that you can be a different person from moment to moment.

26 MONDAY   *Moon Age Day 21 Moon Sign Aquarius*

There is little to stand in your way at the start of this particular week. On the contrary, the lunar high offers you scope to be assertive, enterprising and very cheerful. If your work involves selling, now is the time to push for that mega-deal. On the other hand if your lot in life is to motivate other people, you can certainly earn your crust.

27 TUESDAY   ☿ *Moon Age Day 22 Moon Sign Aquarius*

Properly channelled energies can lead to major successes around now. All that's required is that you don't dissipate your talents and your time. You would also be wise not to commit everything to your work today, but hold back a little so that you have enough energy in reserve to fully enjoy what the evening offers.

28 WEDNESDAY ☿   *Moon Age Day 23 Moon Sign Pisces*

All that glistens certainly isn't gold, as you may be about to discover. Today's events demand that you pay great attention, especially if you are making any sort of decision. It isn't the headlines of life that really matter right now but rather the small print below. Aquarius really does need to keep its eye on the ball.

29 THURSDAY   ☿   *Moon Age Day 24 Moon Sign Pisces*

Good things are possible as far as your romantic life is concerned and if they aren't happening maybe it's because you are not forcing the issue. That little bit of extra effort can make all the difference, and even the way you talk to your lover is extremely important. Always seize the moment in matters of the heart, and especially so now.

30 FRIDAY ☿ *Moon Age Day 25 Moon Sign Aries*

There are signs that you could be getting slightly above yourself in serious debates or even casual discussions. If you think you know what you are talking about, you won't take kindly to anyone who suggests you do not. Rather than getting too uptight about situations, why not allow others to learn by experience?

31 SATURDAY ☿ *Moon Age Day 26 Moon Sign Aries*

Your love life continues to be well starred, and Aquarians who have been looking for new love have scope to find success around now. Venus is in an extremely good position and brings support to your romantic advances, whilst Mars offers the courage and Mercury the mental abilities to sweep someone off their feet.

June

2008

1 SUNDAY ☿ *Moon Age Day 27 Moon Sign Taurus*

Most communication or travel issues can enable you to bring some delight into your life, and if you have planned an early holiday that starts now you could have reason to be glad that you did. Be prepared to use warmth and charm to persuade others to spend some time with you.

2 MONDAY ☿ *Moon Age Day 28 Moon Sign Taurus*

You have the opportunity to get on extremely well in all practical matters today, and to make up your mind quickly at every turn. Your nature remains delightful and with great charm at your disposal there is little that should be denied to you today. This might be the best time of the new month to ask for a raise or promotion.

3 TUESDAY ☿ *Moon Age Day 29 Moon Sign Gemini*

Even if not everything goes your way when it matters the most, you have what it takes to come up with the sort of ideas that lead to eventual success. If others are placing a good deal of responsibility on your shoulders, your best response is to take such things very much in your stride.

4 WEDNESDAY ☿ *Moon Age Day 0 Moon Sign Gemini*

Single Aquarians need to keep an eye out today, mainly because you could well have an admirer you either didn't suspect or who you have dismissed in the past. Few people could fail to notice that you are around if you are keeping up a very public persona, and it's possible that someone is quite smitten by you.

5 THURSDAY   ☿   *Moon Age Day 1 Moon Sign Cancer*

Be careful today because there are signs that you are filled with your own ideas – a state of affairs that might mean you ignore those of anyone else. That's fine, but there may be moments when you have to rely on colleagues or friends and they won't be so willing to help you out if you haven't co-operated.

6 FRIDAY   ☿   *Moon Age Day 2 Moon Sign Cancer*

Keeping up with the Joneses is not really something that appeals much to the average Aquarian, but it might be the case just now. Be careful how far you go because when you are fully back to normal it may upset you to think that you went to any lengths at all just to be like someone else. To Aquarius it is originality that really counts.

7 SATURDAY   ☿   *Moon Age Day 3 Moon Sign Leo*

The weekend brings its own particular ups and downs. The ups are most likely going to be represented by the affection and interest you can attract from other people, whilst the downs are going to be brought by the lunar low and display themselves as a much quieter and more introspective phase for most Aquarians.

8 SUNDAY   ☿   *Moon Age Day 4 Moon Sign Leo*

If you feel slightly restricted by circumstances, you may decide not to start anything new or particularly inspirational for now. Many Aquarians will be quite happy to find somewhere beautiful to be and to simply enjoy the summer weather. Some of you may go no further today than the end of your own garden!

9 MONDAY   ☿   *Moon Age Day 5 Moon Sign Leo*

If there are any limitations being placed upon you right now these are likely to come from external sources, and have little or nothing to do with your own thoughts or actions. All the same you are well equipped to deal with them and can easily turn up the power of your charisma in order to get others to help you out.

10 TUESDAY ☿ *Moon Age Day 6 Moon Sign Virgo*

Stand by to pursue an even more hectic social life, and don't restrict yourself too much whilst such good trends are around. You have what it takes at the moment to make hay whilst the sun shines, both in a practical sense and with regard to more personal matters. A day to stay away from dull people or those who try to hold you back.

11 WEDNESDAY ☿ *Moon Age Day 7 Moon Sign Virgo*

This is a period to make new friends and to influence the ones you have to a greater extent. Even if much of your time is given over to making those around you happy, you may not register the fact because you are having a good time yourself. Almost everything is a matter of involvement and co-operation for Aquarius now.

12 THURSDAY ☿ *Moon Age Day 8 Moon Sign Libra*

The higher the profile you keep, the greater are the potential rewards you can achieve. All the same, there may be just a small part of you that feels slightly more introspective, and this side of your nature needs catering for as well. Even the odd hour spent doing something quiet and reflective could make you feel more complete.

13 FRIDAY ☿ *Moon Age Day 9 Moon Sign Libra*

Good news may now be found in unexpected places, and even if most facets of your life are now settled and happy, there can still be a quiet discontent inside you. For some Aquarians the trouble could be that you are not spreading your wings enough in a physical sense. Maybe you need to travel more?

14 SATURDAY ☿ *Moon Age Day 10 Moon Sign Scorpio*

It's all very well speaking out and letting people know how you feel, but there may be moments today when it would be more advantageous and wiser to simply keep your counsel. This doesn't mean you have to tell any lies and in any case you are not in a particularly contentious frame of mind at present. Friends prove their worth today.

15 SUNDAY ☿ *Moon Age Day 11 Moon Sign Scorpio*

You can afford to let social interests expand and fill more of your life. With a few practical matters left on hold for Sunday you needn't waste the opportunities for personal enjoyment that stand all around you. This may mean getting necessary chores out of the way very early in the day and then setting out to have fun!

16 MONDAY ☿ *Moon Age Day 12 Moon Sign Scorpio*

Going down the same old path this week could seem tedious, and may not get you far in any case. It would be better at present to ring the changes, both at work and with regard to your personal and social life. Getting others to fall in line with your new plans could be a work of art, but if anyone can do it at the moment, you can.

17 TUESDAY ☿ *Moon Age Day 13 Moon Sign Sagittarius*

Financial issues might be rather complex to deal with under present planetary trends and you might need the input of someone more knowledgeable in order to sort things out. Be prepared to find time today for anyone close to you who needs help, or cheering up.

18 WEDNESDAY ☿ *Moon Age Day 14 Moon Sign Sagittarius*

Your ability to convince others today is highlighted, and you can get others to follow your lead in a fairly instinctive way. You have an arresting personality at the best of times but it really seems to shine out at the moment. For this reason you can make yourself the star attraction – a position you cope with incredibly well!

19 THURSDAY ☿ *Moon Age Day 15 Moon Sign Capricorn*

It's worth taking time out to deal with any financial or personal pressures that have been building up for a few days. With only a little effort you can turn things around and show yourself to be truly the master of your own destiny. The admiration you can attract helps you to stay on some sort of pedestal most of the time.

20 FRIDAY   ☿ *Moon Age Day 16 Moon Sign Capricorn*

You have a chance to slow things down, thanks to the presence of the Moon in your solar twelfth house. This encourages you to be more contemplative and slightly less inclined to chase rainbows, no matter how promising they might look. A day to be quite content with your own company.

21 SATURDAY   *Moon Age Day 17 Moon Sign Capricorn*

This has potential to be a varied sort of day, when others may have more confidence in you than you maintain in yourself. You should also stand by for a real boost to energy levels that comes later in the day when the Moon moves into your solar first house and therefore into Aquarius. An evening of fun is on offer.

22 SUNDAY   *Moon Age Day 18 Moon Sign Aquarius*

You now have vitality and self-assurance, which is one of the reasons why others should be so instinctively attracted to you. Aquarius has been generally positive during 2008, and this period of June should be no exception. Whilst others think about doing things that might profit them eventually, you can get busy right now.

23 MONDAY   *Moon Age Day 19 Moon Sign Aquarius*

Your ability to convince other people that you know what you are talking about is very much emphasised today. Don't hold back, and be willing to go that extra mile in order to get what you want. In particular some Aquarians have scope to find the potential partner of their dreams if they keep up the necessary efforts at present.

24 TUESDAY   *Moon Age Day 20 Moon Sign Pisces*

Make the most of rewarding emotional experiences and accept that you can become flavour of the month as far as some colleagues and superiors are concerned. Maintaining your present position, high on that pedestal, can be a wobbly experience at times, but if anyone can keep their balance it's certain that Aquarius can.

25 WEDNESDAY — *Moon Age Day 21 Moon Sign Pisces*

With a firm resolve for self-improvement and a genuine desire to be a better person, trends assist you to embark on new regimes of one sort or another. There's nothing wrong with this unless you set your sights too high in the first place. Be modest in your proposals, fair in your self-estimation and amused by any little failures.

26 THURSDAY — *Moon Age Day 22 Moon Sign Pisces*

If there is any restlessness in your neck of the woods today, it could well be coming directly from you. Not everything may be working out strictly as you might have wished and this can be particularly the case with regard to family matters. In some respects you might feel like that little Dutch boy with his finger in the dam.

27 FRIDAY — *Moon Age Day 23 Moon Sign Aries*

Your mind could be filled with good ideas, though your stamina could be having difficulty keeping up with them all. It would be easier today to follow the ideas and instincts of others for a while, even if this means letting something lapse. Even Aquarius can run out of steam occasionally, particularly if you have been keeping up a frightening pace.

28 SATURDAY — *Moon Age Day 24 Moon Sign Aries*

Even if you are still driven towards change, it's worth recognising that there are certain facets of your life that are best left exactly as they are. This is the dichotomy in which you find yourself. Part of your nature is committed to knocking down the old and rebuilding it, but another part says that maybe conservation is better.

29 SUNDAY — *Moon Age Day 25 Moon Sign Taurus*

It is quite possible that you will be getting yourself involved in discussions or even arguments today simply for the sake of the exercise, and if this is the case you need to be quite careful. Even if you remain convinced that you are correct in most of your assumptions, there could well be times when you are plain wrong. Think first today.

30 MONDAY

Moon Age Day 26   Moon Sign Taurus

The last day of June offers you scope to enjoy the benefits of the early summer, to make changes and to travel about more. Anything that seems to hold you to one spot is not likely to be tolerated at present and you could well be restless to get on. Be prepared to respond to the needs of those around you.

July

2008

1 TUESDAY
Moon Age Day 27 Moon Sign Gemini

When it comes to professional disagreements today it might be better to acquiesce rather than to get involved in situations that could so easily get out of hand. Those higher up the tree might not be too tolerant of your potential interference, even if you know for certain that you are much better informed than they are.

2 WEDNESDAY
Moon Age Day 28 Moon Sign Gemini

Close, emotional relationships work better for you today than casual encounters, so you may well decide to commit yourself to home and family. Not everything is easy to understand under present planetary trends, and this is certainly true in terms of the thought processes and actions of some intimates.

3 THURSDAY
Moon Age Day 0 Moon Sign Cancer

The need to be on the move is highlighted at present and you may not take kindly to being restricted in your actions. If you have the sort of job that ties you to one spot, it's worth finding ways to vary your routines, or boredom is bound to set in. On the other hand if you are retired or presently on holiday, the sky is the limit.

4 FRIDAY
Moon Age Day 1 Moon Sign Cancer

You have scope to fufil your emotional needs through your partner or lover on this particular day, and indeed you could find many people to be especially attentive and kind. Much of this has to do with your own positive attitude and reflects the care and concern that you are able to push out into the world at large. Kindness is the key now.

5 SATURDAY
Moon Age Day 2 Moon Sign Leo

Self-restraint would be no bad thing when it comes to tedious tasks, which could frustrate you whilst the lunar low is around. The more variety you get into your weekend routines, the less you will notice the negative possibilities. At the same time you may restrict yourself from too much running around.

6 SUNDAY
Moon Age Day 3 Moon Sign Leo

It may be time to slow things down, particularly if your general spirits and vitality are on the wane. This is a very temporary matter because even by tomorrow you can be more adventurous and devil-may-care, but for the moment you need to retrench and think things through. Even friends may not be able to draw you out today.

7 MONDAY
Moon Age Day 4 Moon Sign Virgo

You can give a boost to professional developments today and exercise more in the way of personal choice over what is happening to you at work. If there is plenty going on in a social sense too there is no reason at all why you should be bored or feel restricted. By the evening you may want nothing more than a rest.

8 TUESDAY
Moon Age Day 5 Moon Sign Virgo

Making contact with interesting and agreeable people is what this particular period is all about. Many of the individuals you come across at the moment could have ideas that will appeal to you, and could also be very informative regarding a subject that is close to your own heart. There will probably be little time for orthodoxy or routine today.

9 WEDNESDAY
Moon Age Day 6 Moon Sign Libra

It's time to get rid of outmoded situations and to dump any heavy emotional luggage you have been carrying for quite a while. In most cases this process is easy under present trends, but there are some things you need to leave behind that are not so simple to discard. Be brave, because you will travel lighter and happier as a result.

10 THURSDAY   *Moon Age Day 7 Moon Sign Libra*

Social matters now bring out the best in you and there are significant opportunities on offer between now and the weekend. Why not seek out new people waiting in the wings and alternative ways to look at old situations? If you make a break with certain aspects of the past, excitement floods into the vacuum.

11 FRIDAY   *Moon Age Day 8 Moon Sign Libra*

You may not be on form today, especially when it comes to relationships. It seems that the ordinary things other people do are custom-designed to annoy you, and yet there is nothing essentially different about them. The closer the individual, the less this is going to be the case, so it's worth sticking to intimates at the moment.

12 SATURDAY   *Moon Age Day 9 Moon Sign Scorpio*

You need to keep tuned into life this weekend, and the more intellectual and stimulating things are, the better you should appreciate them. Find something radically different to do today, or do something normal in a very different way. If you don't make an effort, boredom with yourself and life could well be the result.

13 SUNDAY   *Moon Age Day 10 Moon Sign Scorpio*

You are about to enter a fairly up-and-down sort of period when it comes to work trends, though influences on your social and personal life couldn't be better in most cases. It might be worth spending some time today looking ahead and working out ways that you can bring more consistency to professional matters, though it might not be easy.

14 MONDAY   *Moon Age Day 11 Moon Sign Sagittarius*

There could be some fairly heavy demands coming your way, though nothing you can't deal with. If there is a problem it could well come from the direction of colleagues, some of whom are really feeling the pressure. It's one thing sorting your own working life out, but something different altogether carrying other people.

15 TUESDAY   *Moon Age Day 12 Moon Sign Sagittarius*

A day to avoid routines like the plague and to fight for a very different sort of life whenever it proves to be possible. Even tedious tasks can be done in ways that are very Aquarian, which means differently. When you are not doing anything strictly practical, stimulating your imagination can work wonders.

16 WEDNESDAY   *Moon Age Day 13 Moon Sign Sagittarius*

New personalities and hearing about exciting situations can help to enliven you around this time. You have the power to attract really original types because you are one yourself, and you probably won't be all that keen to find yourself alongside exactly the same people telling precisely the same stories.

17 THURSDAY   *Moon Age Day 14 Moon Sign Capricorn*

Getting it right first time can be quite important today, but not necessarily all that easy. The most insignificant details suddenly seem to be very relevant, and you might spend a good deal of time on the minutiae of life. You ought to find moments today during which you can let your mind wander and employ your imagination.

18 FRIDAY   *Moon Age Day 15 Moon Sign Capricorn*

A slightly quieter day is on offer, when it may be difficult to find much excitement. You may decide to spend more time getting things done in a concrete sense, and that is important too. With a twelfth-house Moon your approachable side is not to the fore, and you may be happiest alone.

19 SATURDAY   *Moon Age Day 16 Moon Sign Aquarius*

Acting on impulse and making snap decisions can work wonders now the lunar high is around. All the originality of your nature can now be put on display and you shouldn't have any trouble at all influencing and interesting others. You can afford to take risks and to be both different and quite outrageous at times.

20 SUNDAY   *Moon Age Day 17 Moon Sign Aquarius*

It may be hard to find situations on a Sunday that allow you to outwit the competition or get ahead in a work sense, but you do need to stretch yourself nevertheless. Some Aquarians will be doing so in a sporting way, but most of you will simply be pitting your wits against relatives, friends, or anyone else who will participate.

21 MONDAY   *Moon Age Day 18 Moon Sign Aquarius*

Even if you have the chance to spend more time at home today than would normally be the case on an average Monday, this may not be what you want to do. The lunar high is still around for most of the day, encouraging you to do something different and make youself quite hypnotic to other people.

22 TUESDAY   *Moon Age Day 19 Moon Sign Pisces*

You can seek out real support today from people who seem to matter a great deal. Actually sorting out the wheat from the chaff isn't quite that easy though, and you needn't accept help from everyone – particularly not those who have a vested interest in seeing you behave in a specific way. Self-choices are the ones that now count.

23 WEDNESDAY   *Moon Age Day 20 Moon Sign Pisces*

There is a danger of you being rather full of yourself right now, and your own ego could be your undoing if you don't exercise just a little care and show some humility. It isn't often that Aquarius becomes arrogant, but extra care is necessary right now – no matter how good you are at doing something.

24 THURSDAY   *Moon Age Day 21 Moon Sign Aries*

The more you are able to broaden your mental horizons, the greater can be your overall enjoyment of life at the moment. You can persuade even the most unlikely people to give you great support and new ideas, often without realising that they are doing anything at all. Even snippets of conversation are also grist to your mill today.

25 FRIDAY
Moon Age Day 22 Moon Sign Aries

You should still not be dissuaded from following your own path or from doing something that seems more important to you than it does to your friends or colleagues. Even when you are out there on your own you are able to make headway, and in any case it is sometimes vitally important to rely absolutely on yourself.

26 SATURDAY
Moon Age Day 23 Moon Sign Taurus

In a direct contrast to yesterday you can now gain much more from being in co-operative situations and from finding yourself involved with ventures that are of a very community-based sort. You can afford to give at least part of this weekend in service to others and to good causes. Be prepared to show your caring side.

27 SUNDAY
Moon Age Day 24 Moon Sign Taurus

Even if you still intend to get what you want from life, your efforts are now much more likely to be geared towards the general good and not simply your own. This allows you to feel much more comfortable because deep inside you have a very moral and socially motivated core. Make time today to spoil your partner.

28 MONDAY
Moon Age Day 25 Moon Sign Gemini

Certain hold-ups may be unavoidable today, and this might not be the most exciting start you have had to any particular week. Take problems in your stride and sort out muddles one at a time. Humour is the key now, and that will please you no end because you are a natural joker and relish having a laugh.

29 TUESDAY
Moon Age Day 26 Moon Sign Gemini

What could be a slight irritant today is making others understand exactly what you are trying to say. A time of slight pressures is possible, when it seems as if some of your objectives are both difficult to achieve and even awkward to envisage. Rather than changing direction just yet, why not wait until things settle?

30 WEDNESDAY   *Moon Age Day 27 Moon Sign Cancer*

You would be wise to take precautions before you embark on any sort of risk, especially when it comes to your money. It might be better to avoid putting yourself in the firing line at all today, because you probably work better on your own for the moment. Socially speaking you can remain on form, but might be happiest with good friends.

31 THURSDAY   *Moon Age Day 28 Moon Sign Cancer*

You can make this a good day if you keep on the move – and the further you are able to go the better you should feel. Anything that enlarges your view of life ahead of the lunar low has got to be considered positive, and you probably won't take kindly to being restricted in your movements or to being bullied into conforming.

August 2008

1 FRIDAY
Moon Age Day 0 Moon Sign Leo

If there are differences of opinion around today, your best response is to avoid getting involved at all. The Moon is in Leo, which is the lunar low for you, and this is not a good time to be arguing with anyone. The more relaxed and sedate you can remain, the greater is the chance that you will feel happy with your present lot in life.

2 SATURDAY
Moon Age Day 1 Moon Sign Leo

Personal freedoms remain as important to you as they have been over the last few weeks but this may not be the best day of the month on which to pursue them. Be prepared to keep a low profile, stick to doing those things you know you can accomplish easily and don't make waves. By tomorrow you can make sure things are far more dynamic.

3 SUNDAY
Moon Age Day 2 Moon Sign Virgo

Suddenly you can release yourself from pressures that are quite difficult to recognise. All you know is that you have more scope to share yourself with the world at large. Disappointments are less likely now and you can definitely find ways in which to pep up the pace of your own life and that of friends who have been out of sorts.

4 MONDAY
Moon Age Day 3 Moon Sign Virgo

Differences of opinion that arise, most probably at work, could lead to arguments, most of which are not at all necessary. Withdrawing from situations of confrontation might be best, even if you don't really want to do so. As far as your social life is concerned it looks as though you can make almost anything happen on this particular week.

121

5 TUESDAY
Moon Age Day 4 Moon Sign Virgo

You are in a position to attract much goodwill from the direction of your friends today. Make use of this fact by allowing them to help you with something that has bothered you for a few days or more. Trends encourage a search for luxury this week, though you may have to look hard for it.

6 WEDNESDAY
Moon Age Day 5 Moon Sign Libra

Your optimism should be on the increase – not that there is anything strange about an optimistic Aquarian. In particular you can afford to look towards the possibilities that could come from travel, and to take any opportunity this month to change your surroundings. Even if relatives don't co-operate today, you can get friends to do so.

7 THURSDAY
Moon Age Day 6 Moon Sign Libra

New opportunities to get ahead are there for the taking via your career, and in the case of some Aquarians a change of job is a distinct possibility quite soon. This is a day that works better for you if you keep your eyes open because most of the benefits you can achieve are a result of your own intervention.

8 FRIDAY
Moon Age Day 7 Moon Sign Scorpio

If anything takes the wind out of your sails at the moment it may well be the way colleagues or some friends are behaving. Of course they have their own interests at heart but even allowing for that you could face some selfishness. Rather than responding in kind, why not focus your attention on a fulfilling social life?

9 SATURDAY
Moon Age Day 8 Moon Sign Scorpio

If at all possible you need to opt for a complete change of scenery today. There are gains to be made from altering some of your perspectives, and this is easier if you look at them from an entirely different place. In addition, if you have been working hard of late, a short break would do you no end of good.

10 SUNDAY *Moon Age Day 9 Moon Sign Sagittarius*

Be prepared to seek the support you need today from your partner and family members. Chances are you have been so busy just living your life of late that you haven't paid as much attention to those you love as you should have done. Today offers you the chance to redress that balance and to put things right.

11 MONDAY *Moon Age Day 10 Moon Sign Sagittarius*

Getting exactly what you want might not prove to be all that easy at the start of this week, particularly if you are tied down by responsibilities and rules of one sort or another. It might be best to avoid some of these altogether by retreating from some of the responsibilities – if only for today.

12 TUESDAY *Moon Age Day 11 Moon Sign Sagittarius*

There is now a strong emphasis on keeping what is yours, even to the extent of being less generous and giving to friends. This sort of selfishness runs completely counter to your basic nature and is an effect of present planetary trends. It is something you need to work against during the next couple of days at least.

13 WEDNESDAY *Moon Age Day 12 Moon Sign Capricorn*

Even if your confidence remains reasonably high, you work better now when you know that there is support around you. This can be gained from a number of different directions, but is especially important when it emanates from your partner. All forms of co-operation offer you scope to be particularly comfortable and content.

14 THURSDAY *Moon Age Day 13 Moon Sign Capricorn*

Going it alone is still not your best approach, and it's worth seeking some support if you need it. Your social life is highlighted during most of this month, despite moments when friends prove to be somewhat fickle and when their actions leave you feeling left out in the cold.

15 FRIDAY   *Moon Age Day 14 Moon Sign Aquarius*

The lunar high allows you to move closer to your heart's desire today and tomorrow than at any other time during August. You can easily persuade others to follow your lead and should be less insecure – for a while at least. Most important of all, your ability to attract good luck means that you can afford to take a few more chances.

16 SATURDAY   *Moon Age Day 15 Moon Sign Aquarius*

Now you have scope to race ahead, and if you are not then chances are you are failing to put in that extra bit of effort that can make all the difference. What really counts at the moment is your willingness to have a go – even at things you haven't done before. Anything especially unusual has potential to get your attention now.

17 SUNDAY   *Moon Age Day 16 Moon Sign Aquarius*

You have what it takes to stand up for your rights today, together with those of the people you love. So forceful is your nature that you needn't let others get in your way. This doesn't mean you are going to be argumentative or unpleasant. On the contrary, you can get almost anything you want and still remain charming.

18 MONDAY   *Moon Age Day 17 Moon Sign Pisces*

Now is the time to take any opportunity to improve your lot at work, and for some Aquarians this could mean thinking about a total change of career. If you know you haven't been appreciated as much as you should have been during the last few months the time, why not speak out and try to improve things?

19 TUESDAY   *Moon Age Day 18 Moon Sign Pisces*

There is more you can do to further your potential and to show a sometimes unsuspecting world what you are capable of doing. Don't sell yourself short in any situation and be willing to go that extra mile in order to achieve your objectives. Today can also be particularly interesting and important with regard to love.

20 WEDNESDAY   *Moon Age Day 19 Moon Sign Aries*

The impact of your personality can be very strong right now, and you may even cause others to take a sharp intake of breath on occasion. Some of your more grandiose plans may have to be tempered a little, not because they won't work, but merely so you can get others to follow your lead.

21 THURSDAY   *Moon Age Day 20 Moon Sign Aries*

There are signs that what you want to do more than anything else at the moment is to form ever more ambitious plans for the future, but be careful because this might mean ignoring something that definitely should be done right now. Rather than arguing with awkward types, be prepared to try to understand them.

22 FRIDAY   *Moon Age Day 21 Moon Sign Taurus*

The focus is on competitiveness, and you may be unwilling to accept second place if you know that with just a little extra effort you can stand on the winners podium. This can apply to almost any facet of your life and certainly isn't restricted to sporting activities. You might also be very community-minded now.

23 SATURDAY   *Moon Age Day 22 Moon Sign Taurus*

Uncompleted tasks can now be finished off – especially those that have a bearing on your home life and the level of your comfort for some weeks or months to come. A slightly quieter weekend is possible, offering a chance to stay around the homestead and tackle jobs that you have ignored recently.

24 SUNDAY   *Moon Age Day 23 Moon Sign Gemini*

You have what it takes to talk to almost anyone and this gift of the gab is greater at the moment than is usually the case, even for Aquarius. It is through communicating with others that you get what you want and need from life, so it is not a gift that should be underestimated. Soon you may be talking to someone extremely important.

25 MONDAY
Moon Age Day 24 Moon Sign Gemini

Standard responses may not work at the start of this working week, and you might have to work hard to get others to follow your lead and to accept what you are saying without question. This brings an element of challenge into your life and that is something you relish. When it comes to your love life, a demonstrative approach works well.

26 TUESDAY
Moon Age Day 25 Moon Sign Gemini

At the present time you know how to work diligently and to move fairly steadily towards your chosen goals in life. That doesn't mean you appear dull to others, but it does infer that you can avoid some of the flippancy that might have attended your life on occasion across the last few weeks. You are gradually hardening yourself up somewhat.

27 WEDNESDAY
Moon Age Day 26 Moon Sign Cancer

Friendship proves to be very important right now and you have what it takes to do anything you can to support a pal who is having problems. Don't be at all surprised if you are asked to do something that could cause you a little anxiety. Just do your best because nobody can expect more than that.

28 THURSDAY
Moon Age Day 27 Moon Sign Cancer

When it comes to getting on well in your career it seems to be the case at the moment that flattering the right people can do you a great deal of good. It doesn't cost you anything to be pleasant, and even if you have to tell the odd white lie, fortune will forgive you. Once you achieve your objectives you can be as truthful as you like!

29 FRIDAY
Moon Age Day 28 Moon Sign Leo

It looks as though you are still able to get on especially well with superiors or people who have it in their power to help you get on in some way. There are quieter times on offer today, brought about by the lunar low, but because of a powerful Mars in your solar chart the Moon's effect should be quite limited this time around.

30 SATURDAY
Moon Age Day 29 Moon Sign Leo

The start of the weekend might be quiet, but if so it is because you want things that way. Providence continues to smile on you and it shouldn't be difficult for you to be in the right place at the most opportune time. All the lunar low seems to do is to take some of the gold off the gingerbread when you do make a success.

31 SUNDAY
Moon Age Day 0 Moon Sign Virgo

Acting on impulse is almost a way of life to Aquarius, but probably less so now and over the days and weeks to come. Even if you are as much fun as ever, it's worth hardening your attitude towards your own future and avoiding taking as many things for granted as sometimes turns out to be the case.

September

2008

1 MONDAY
Moon Age Day 1 Moon Sign Virgo

What works best this week is to surround yourself with the right sort of people on each specific occasion. At work you need to be amongst the go-getters and pace-makers, whilst in a social sense you are best off with more compliant and easy-going sorts. In terms of your personal life, all you really need is that one special person.

2 TUESDAY
Moon Age Day 2 Moon Sign Libra

There is no doubt about it, you love to be in the social mainstream at the moment and have what it takes to get yourself noticed. Be prepared to get on your glad rags and cause a sharp intake of breath from people you meet, since your personal magnetism is presently going off the scale. Let's face it – Aquarius is sizzling!

3 WEDNESDAY
Moon Age Day 3 Moon Sign Libra

Trends support a degree of moodiness and a tendency to fall out with people about the most inconsequential matters. It would be a shame to spoil the party just for the sake of a quick passing trend, and you can avoid doing so by counting to ten before you say something you will regret later.

4 THURSDAY
Moon Age Day 4 Moon Sign Scorpio

What you shouldn't lack at this point in time is self-belief and you can afford to approach your life more like a Fire-sign individual than the Air-sign type that you actually are. There's nothing wrong with confidence, but you have to remember that your follow-through isn't always impeccable, and you could end up with egg on your face.

5 FRIDAY
Moon Age Day 5 Moon Sign Scorpio

It's great to have pleasant people around you, and you have scope to achieve this right now. What a great week this could turn out to be for Aquarians who have decided to take a holiday, but even if you are stuck in your usual rut you can find ways to ring the changes enough to feel quite content with your lot.

6 SATURDAY
Moon Age Day 6 Moon Sign Scorpio

An ideal time to make contact with people you don't see or speak to very often. Failing that, you may decide to get out and about and see something new for the weekend. Finally, if you have no choice but to stop at home on your own, why not search out a really good book?

7 SUNDAY
Moon Age Day 7 Moon Sign Sagittarius

Even if there are slight restrictions placed upon your movements today, you should manage to get through or round these quite easily. You can be especially good in conversation at present, and although talking to others is never a problem to you, right now you have scope to be positively eloquent!

8 MONDAY
Moon Age Day 8 Moon Sign Sagittarius

Your expectations today could be slightly higher than proves to be sensible, and you would be well advised to check and recheck all details before proceeding. Life won't let you down just as long as you put in that extra bit of effort that can make all the difference. If in doubt you should call on the help of an expert.

9 TUESDAY
Moon Age Day 9 Moon Sign Capricorn

Interesting gatherings help you to bring out the best in yourself, and might allow you to make good headway in practical as well as strictly social matters. Mixing business with pleasure is not difficult under present planetary trends and you appear to have what it takes to push the bounds of the possible even more than usual.

10 WEDNESDAY   *Moon Age Day 10 Moon Sign Capricorn*

Much of the real joy you can achieve at the moment comes from what you can do for others rather than as a result of what you manage to do for yourself. The focus is on your selfless attitude, and on your love and compassion, even towards people who may not have been universally kind to you in the past.

11 THURSDAY   *Moon Age Day 11 Moon Sign Capricorn*

It's one thing assuming that you are right about something but quite another to push the issue to such an extent that you fall out with someone. Even if you continue to be attentive and kind, you may also be rather too emphatic for your own good right now. Just bear in mind that there is always an alternative point of view.

12 FRIDAY   *Moon Age Day 12 Moon Sign Aquarius*

This might be a good time to look at career choices and to make certain changes if you feel these are necessary. Some of these may involve you looking not weeks but months or even years ahead, and this is often difficult for Aquarius, who is a child of the moment. All the same, a concrete and definite life-plan is certainly in order.

13 SATURDAY   *Moon Age Day 13 Moon Sign Aquarius*

Today the lunar high is less practical and more personal in the way it has a bearing on your life. Now your concern with thinking way ahead is best replaced with a wish to make life better and more exciting today. Find ways to get others involved in your plans and set out to have a good time. This evening could be especially noteworthy.

14 SUNDAY   *Moon Age Day 14 Moon Sign Pisces*

It seems as though your personal and domestic life now takes centre-stage, encouraging you to find more time to get on side with family members who could have been rather distant of late. Today is also ideal for travelling to see someone who you care for deeply but who you definitely don't see every day.

15 MONDAY
Moon Age Day 15 Moon Sign Pisces

New doors open this week, but that won't help you at all if you refuse to peer through them to see what is on the other side. Curiosity is a great thing and you usually have plenty, but just now you might have to tease yourself into greater investigations. The progress you make today depends almost entirely on the effort you put in.

16 TUESDAY
Moon Age Day 16 Moon Sign Aries

Right now love issues could turn out to be far too dramatic and emotional for your liking. Even if this isn't coming from your direction, you are subject to it all the same. Some Aquarians will therefore be trying to keep lovers at arms length for a while, or else choosing to mix with those who are friends rather than intimates.

17 WEDNESDAY
Moon Age Day 17 Moon Sign Aries

Associates and particularly colleagues could let you down around now, which is why you have to be on the ball and paying attention all through the working day. The same is less likely to be the case with regard to friends, who should be reliable and trustworthy. The real problem comes with colleagues who are also your pals.

18 THURSDAY
Moon Age Day 18 Moon Sign Aries

Where new professional developments are concerned, trends assist you to keep your finger on the pulse, and you shouldn't have many problems keeping up with new incentives and possibilities. Today would also be good for a shopping spree, especially if you can combine it with a social get-together.

19 FRIDAY
Moon Age Day 19 Moon Sign Taurus

You can get most of what is happening in the practical world to go your way now, and you shouldn't have to pay attention all the time in order to zoom in on what is going to help you out today and across the coming weekend. What you would be wise to concentrate on for the next few days is the way your love life is panning out.

20 SATURDAY   *Moon Age Day 20 Moon Sign Taurus*

It's worth tuning in to the needs of your partner or significant other. There is less emotional tension around and a more relaxed atmosphere that proves to be both happy and fulfilling. Whereas it might have appeared that everything you did before was wrong to your lover, now you can make sure you are flavour of the month.

21 SUNDAY   *Moon Age Day 21 Moon Sign Gemini*

There is no need for double-checking or too much caution today if you know instinctively what you ought to do and how it should be undertaken. The practical aspects of life may not be too important in any case because a definite overview works best, as does leaving the intricate details to more fussy types.

22 MONDAY   *Moon Age Day 22 Moon Sign Gemini*

If something important needs discussing, you could hardly choose a more suitable day than this one. By keeping your approach casual but attentive, you can avoid falling out with anyone. Such is your present charm that you could easily get on side with someone who is usually about as prickly as a cactus.

23 TUESDAY   *Moon Age Day 23 Moon Sign Cancer*

There is just a slight possibility today that you will become so enmeshed in your own ideas and dreams that you tend to forget those of someone who is very important to you. Only a slight modification is necessary to accommodate that very special person, and the results should be more than worth any effort you have to put in.

24 WEDNESDAY   *Moon Age Day 24 Moon Sign Cancer*

You have scope to enjoy the company of many different sorts of people out here in the middle of the week, and may not want to concentrate too much on any one of your friends. You can also find ways to incorporate your more emotional attachments with those that are far more casual. Your desire to make everyone as happy as possible is to the fore.

25 THURSDAY ☿ *Moon Age Day 25 Moon Sign Leo*

The lunar low arrives, encouraging you to put the brakes on somewhat. It isn't that you can't make any progress today and tomorrow, merely that you might have to keep stopping in order to check what you have already done. A quieter and less inspired Aquarius is likely today

26 FRIDAY ☿ *Moon Age Day 26 Moon Sign Leo*

A lull is in place and there may be little you can do except show a little patience and wait for tomorrow. Now is the time to take things slowly and try to get enjoyment not out of what you do but the way you undertake it. The more contemplative you are, the greater will be the rewards you get from this less than exciting day.

27 SATURDAY ☿ *Moon Age Day 27 Moon Sign Virgo*

The one advantage of the lunar low is the way you can respond when it disappears. As the Moon moves on you should find yourself facing a weekend that seems somewhat more exciting than it actually is. Nevertheless, you can make the most of any opportunity that comes your way and should enjoy being with others.

28 SUNDAY ☿ *Moon Age Day 28 Moon Sign Virgo*

Once again you might have to tread rather carefully in terms of emotional attachments. Is it that your lover doesn't understand you, or that you find them difficult to fathom? The answer is that there are likely to be slight misunderstandings on both sides, but these can easily be overcome with just a little mutual effort.

29 MONDAY ☿ *Moon Age Day 29 Moon Sign Libra*

As a new week gets started you could well decide that you want to move away from any sort of intensity or emotional upheaval. There is a strong desire to keep things light and airy and a definite need for something new to take your interest. Sometimes you see aspects of your life more clearly from a distance.

30 TUESDAY ☿ *Moon Age Day 0 Moon Sign Libra*

The focus is on keen judgement at work and a strong desire to have things right at home ahead of the upcoming winter. Maybe you are opting for a decorating spree or replacing certain furnishings. Whatever decisions you make, it's worth bearing in mind any long-term consequences, particularly financial ones.

October

2008

1 WEDNESDAY ☿ *Moon Age Day 1 Moon Sign Libra*

The first day of October offers you scope to look towards your social life with renewed vigour and a determination to make things more exciting. You can't go for long at a time without pepping things up in one way or another, and today would be an ideal time to plan for a very special sort of happening at the weekend.

2 THURSDAY ☿ *Moon Age Day 2 Moon Sign Scorpio*

Today's influences are not of the best sort for clear-headed planning, and there might be occasions when you find yourself baffled by things that normally wouldn't confuse you at all. You need time out to resolve issues and shouldn't get so carried away with half a dozen jobs that you fail to do any one of them to the best of your ability.

3 FRIDAY ☿ *Moon Age Day 3 Moon Sign Scorpio*

Make the most of the good things happening around you, even if you are not directly involved in everything. When it comes to personal enjoyment you may decide to wait until the evening, particularly if you remain extremely busy from a practical point of view. Routines can seem extremely tedious at times and are best avoided.

4 SATURDAY ☿ *Moon Age Day 4 Moon Sign Sagittarius*

In terms of your personality you can dominate most proceedings across the weekend and that could start very early on today. Why not spend some time with friends if you can, and keep your day bright and breezy? This is probably not the right time for serious conversations or for trying to sort out the whys and wherefores of the world.

5 SUNDAY ☿ *Moon Age Day 5 Moon Sign Sagittarius*

By all means keep plugging away at home, getting things the way you want them to be for the weeks and months ahead, but at the same time you need to please yourself socially too. You may not be at your most patient today, and casual attachments, together with instant and not too important happenings might suit you best.

6 MONDAY ☿ *Moon Age Day 6 Moon Sign Sagittarius*

Trends assist any Aquarians who have been feeling slightly out of sorts across the last few days to feel a good deal better. There is certainly likely to be a more positive attitude available from the world at large, and some of those things you have wanted to do for a while but were restricted from completing are now possible.

7 TUESDAY ☿ *Moon Age Day 7 Moon Sign Capricorn*

It's worth having a close look at any new moneymaking projects, because you can't dismiss everything without examination. Someone rather special might be coming into your life around this time, maybe a celebrity or a person you have worshipped from afar. What follows could be very interesting indeed.

8 WEDNESDAY ☿ *Moon Age Day 8 Moon Sign Capricorn*

You can be intriguing and intrigued today – it's a two-way process. Almost anything can captivate your curiosity and imagination, and at the same time you have what it takes to fascinate others. What are you doing to engender these strange reactions? Nothing at all except being a fairly typical Aquarian subject.

9 THURSDAY ☿ *Moon Age Day 9 Moon Sign Aquarius*

The lunar high offers one of the strong points of the month and will almost certainly allow you a greater sense of freedom, self-choice and potential success. It isn't as if money is being handed to you in buckets, but you do now have a greater sense of purpose and a really good ability to sniff out some genuine advantages.

10 FRIDAY ☿ *Moon Age Day 10 Moon Sign Aquarius*

You can continue to get things going well for you, and with an upturn in general fortunes comes an improvement in your mental attitude. What before seemed impossible now only appears slightly difficult and what used to be hard is now routine. Your mental capacity is especially well starred, and likely to remain so for much of this month.

11 SATURDAY ☿ *Moon Age Day 11 Moon Sign Aquarius*

For the third day in a row the Moon is in Aquarius, helping you to stay on top form. There may be some personal situations around today that you may want to avoid, probably by refusing to talk about them, but in the main you can make significant progress and ought to feel generally good with your lot in life.

12 SUNDAY ☿ *Moon Age Day 12 Moon Sign Pisces*

This could turn out to be one of the most progressive Sundays you will experience during the autumn. You have a greater than average capacity to keep going, well after others have fallen by the wayside. There are advantages on offer that you may not have previously suspected, but the important thing is that you react quickly.

13 MONDAY ☿ *Moon Age Day 13 Moon Sign Pisces*

A break from routine might be necessary this week, even if you are hedged around by the everyday necessities and responsibilities of life. How you can ring the changes and yet still do what is expected of you is going to be your homework for the first part of the week, but if anyone can find a way, Aquarius certainly can!

14 TUESDAY ☿ *Moon Age Day 14 Moon Sign Aries*

The general state of romance improves under present planetary trends and that helps you to find wonderful company and to say exactly the right things to deepen an existing attachment or to form one in the first place. You are rarely stuck for words, but just at present they should drip from your tongue like honey.

15 WEDNESDAY ☿   *Moon Age Day 15 Moon Sign Aries*

Some busy preparation is called for, and there may not be time to scratch your nose today if you want to make the very best of what is around you. If you are approaching the end of a particular task or sequence of jobs that has been going on for some time, why not get your head around what you are going to tackle next?

16 THURSDAY ☿   *Moon Age Day 16 Moon Sign Taurus*

It has to be said that there are times when a tried and tested approach is the best one to adopt, though you sometimes don't realise the fact. Everything in your life is change and originality – that's just the way you are. Nevertheless, if you don't follow an expected path today you could be brought firmly down to earth with a bump.

17 FRIDAY   *Moon Age Day 17 Moon Sign Taurus*

Romantic plans might have to be changed at short notice – not that this need bother you too much because you are used to thinking on your feet. It could be that you have blundered without realising, and so might have to make a few apologies before you can get your usual level of co-operation from others and from your lover especially.

18 SATURDAY   *Moon Age Day 18 Moon Sign Gemini*

Whilst others get all complicated about solving little problems, you can have them sorted in no time at all. This is the sort of behaviour that gets you noticed and especially so under present planetary trends. You barely have to open your mouth today before someone declares you to be a genius. It might not be true, but it is gratifying.

19 SUNDAY   *Moon Age Day 19 Moon Sign Gemini*

Be prepared to keep your ambitions under close scrutiny for the next few days. It isn't that you are any less potentially successful than you usually are, merely that you may be expecting rather too much, even of your skills. Things will go much smoother if you are willing to accept that there are some things you don't know. That might mean seeking help.

20 MONDAY
Moon Age Day 20 Moon Sign Cancer

Most noteworthy of all in your life just now is your creative potential. You should know instinctively what looks and feels right and can really wow people with your sense of style. Add to this a very positive attitude to life and an expression that says you can't believe everyone is not as cool as you are, and success is there for the taking.

21 TUESDAY
Moon Age Day 21 Moon Sign Cancer

Your strength today lies in doing everything you can to support the underdog. If there is one thing you cannot abide it is a bully or people who want to foist their redundant ideas onto everyone else. That's why if you see someone who looks downtrodden today, you can afford to leap to their defence.

22 WEDNESDAY
Moon Age Day 22 Moon Sign Leo

Certain aspects of material progress could be difficult whilst the lunar low is around, and you may not be half so cocksure of yourself as has been the case across the last few days. Nor will speaking out in company be your top priority – in fact it might be far more comfortable to spend as much time as possible on your own.

23 THURSDAY
Moon Age Day 23 Moon Sign Leo

There are no instant solutions around at the moment, and the fact that you can't conjure answers from thin air could really get on your nerves. Fortunately this should be a very temporary phase and one that can't endure much beyond today. Even by this evening you can get back to being much more like your usual self.

24 FRIDAY
Moon Age Day 24 Moon Sign Virgo

There might be very little happening as far as your major ambitions and desires are concerned, and if you are willing to put up with being in the doldrums that's the way things will stay. However, if you inject a little extra effort into your life, circumstances should start to work in your favour. It's all a case of intervening at just the right time.

25 SATURDAY   *Moon Age Day 25 Moon Sign Virgo*

Despite your constant need to alter things at the drop of a hat, it is the stable work patterns and normal actions that bring the greatest potential rewards for the moment. Now is the time to still that butterfly mind and leave some of your originality alone, at least during this weekend. Be receptive to good ideas from others.

26 SUNDAY   *Moon Age Day 26 Moon Sign Virgo*

If you are surrounded by people who are constantly crying wolf, that could make you rather unsettled. It would be best to look at the evidence in any situation yourself and to then make up your own mind rather than relying on the opinions of others. In matters of love an attentive approach works best.

27 MONDAY   *Moon Age Day 27 Moon Sign Libra*

Progress could be significantly slowed at the start of this working week but more because of the actions of other people than on account of anything you are saying or doing. All you can really do is show a degree of patience and to help out whenever it proves to be possible. Fortunately you can make sure your social life is anything but slow.

28 TUESDAY   *Moon Age Day 28 Moon Sign Libra*

Things continue to buzz in terms of the bearing you can have on life outside work. Some Aquarians might be making extended journeys around this time, and if you are one of them you could find things working out even better than you had hoped. Even if you are forced to stick around the same place, you can allow your imagination to travel.

29 WEDNESDAY   *Moon Age Day 0 Moon Sign Scorpio*

The focus is on a strong desire to agree with others and to find a way forward, even where there have been significant difficulties in the past. You might also be particularly good at pouring oil on troubled waters as far as friends are concerned, and can use this to play the honest broker as this week moves on towards its end.

30 THURSDAY   *Moon Age Day 1 Moon Sign Scorpio*

Even if you are now slightly less assertive than was the case earlier in the month, to compensate you can be extremely sensitive, and shouldn't have any problem coming to conclusions that are based on intuition. This puts you one step ahead in certain situations and you would be well advised to follow your instincts most of the time.

31 FRIDAY   *Moon Age Day 2 Moon Sign Sagittarius*

Confidence is still present, even if it sometimes feels as though you are walking a tightrope today. Above all your courage is emphasised, assisting you to face people and situations that have really unnerved you in the past. Even if you quake a little inside, you needn't betray the fact.

November
2008

1 SATURDAY
Moon Age Day 3 Moon Sign Sagittarius

Your personal life could seem vague and complex – that is if you choose to analyse it too much. If you can't resolve all romantic issues just now, maybe you should concentrate instead on less emotional attachments, sticking to friends who want nothing but your company. Don't allow life to get too confusing or awkward.

2 SUNDAY
Moon Age Day 4 Moon Sign Sagittarius

You have scope to capitalise on favourable financial trends. Part of you says that you are involved in pipedreams whilst your deeper reasoning tells you to go ahead. There is no harm in at least exploring these avenues – that is if you tangibly recognise them.

3 MONDAY
Moon Age Day 5 Moon Sign Capricorn

The positive financial influences continue this week, so you need to pay attention and get things right first time. It is also possible for you to benefit from effort you put in previously and as a result of opportunities you may have thought were lost and gone forever.

4 TUESDAY
Moon Age Day 6 Moon Sign Capricorn

Because you are so good to have around you may well be in great demand at the moment. This isn't just a social thing but can extend to other spheres of your life too. When it comes to making a decision that is going to have a bearing on where you will be around this time next year, you may need to make your mind up now.

5 WEDNESDAY
Moon Age Day 7 Moon Sign Aquarius

Things can go from fairly quiet to positively hectic today and you need to be on top form in order to benefit from everything that is on offer. Only an Aquarian would try to do so, but if things look inviting you may not be able to help yourself. Romance is especially well highlighted today, with new understandings developing for some.

6 THURSDAY
Moon Age Day 8 Moon Sign Aquarius

With little time to think things through, much of what you achieve today may be done on automatic pilot. Not that you are especially interested in everyday routines. On the contrary, it is towards the showy and brash side of life that you are encouraged to turn during the lunar high, and why not? Nobody said we have to be serious all the time.

7 FRIDAY
Moon Age Day 9 Moon Sign Aquarius

If ever there was a time to let yourself go and to shock a few people on the way, this is it. Lady Luck is almost certainly on your side and it shouldn't be remotely difficult to make the very best of impressions on practically everyone. For Aquarius the weekend can be started early, and there are fifty different kinds of fun on offer!

8 SATURDAY
Moon Age Day 10 Moon Sign Pisces

Saturday might seem positively pedestrian after the last few days, but in reality you are able to achieve a great deal and can afford to be quite cheerful in the way you go about it. A day to make the most of interactions with family members and also close friends.

9 SUNDAY
Moon Age Day 11 Moon Sign Pisces

You still have scope to be on good form and open to new suggestions and all manner of possibilities. If you are an Aquarian who does not work at the weekend, why not earmark a good part of today to do something radically different? Invitations from friends are well accented under present trends.

10 MONDAY
Moon Age Day 12 Moon Sign Aries

Even if most people are reliable, there may be the odd one or two who are not, and these are the types you have to watch out for at present. Aquarians are not usually the type to be duped, but there could be some very skilled operators around at the moment and they might even take you in. When it comes to getting on at work, be bold.

11 TUESDAY
Moon Age Day 13 Moon Sign Aries

The focus is now on your willingness to put yourself at the disposal of others, both inside and outside of work. Some Aquarians will now be thinking in terms of new interests or hobbies, and if you are one of them, you can afford to move away from the pedestrian and the normal, towards something truly expressive.

12 WEDNESDAY
Moon Age Day 14 Moon Sign Taurus

The time is right to get well on side with those who are on the up. You don't normally use others as a vehicle towards your own success but if their elevator is on the way you might as well hitch a ride. In any case you needn't be just a passenger if you have your own original ideas. These contribute to the lives of colleagues and friends, not just yours.

13 THURSDAY
Moon Age Day 15 Moon Sign Taurus

It is towards your home life that you are encouraged to look today and maybe until the coming weekend. If relatives are especially kind to you right now, suspicious as you are under present planetary trends, you might wonder just what it is they are after. You may be about to find out!

14 FRIDAY
Moon Age Day 16 Moon Sign Gemini

Getting the everyday chores done can seem quite boring today, that is unless you look at them differently. There is nobody better than you for seeking a degree of originality or for discovering methods of work that are interesting as well as useful. You can afford to go through life with a definite skip in your step and a song in your heart now.

15 SATURDAY
Moon Age Day 17 Moon Sign Gemini

It looks as though for a day or two at least you have scope to dispense with your usual idealism, in favour of practical common sense. That works well in most cases, but people who like and trust your nature might feel you have suddenly become much more cynical than usual. Remember the adage, 'moderation in all things'.

16 SUNDAY
Moon Age Day 18 Moon Sign Cancer

Stand by for potential misunderstandings, brought about by a combination of the present position of Mars and Mercury in your solar chart. You simply misconstrue what others are saying and might make silly mistakes at every turn. Don't be alarmed because you can make most of what happens humorous and not serious.

17 MONDAY
Moon Age Day 19 Moon Sign Cancer

When it comes to getting your own way you have a number of weapons in your personal armoury today. Number one is your wonderful nature, which exudes joy and encourages others at every turn. In addition, you can be quite persuasive now, and have what it takes to convince everyone that what you want is also their ideal.

18 TUESDAY
Moon Age Day 20 Moon Sign Leo

The lunar low might slow you down a little, but it needn't prevent the general momentum you have built up in your life as a whole. Don't let anyone lord it over you at present and be prepared to stick up for yourself, even if you are not absolutely sure of the ground upon which you stand. Support from others can be sought later.

19 WEDNESDAY
Moon Age Day 21 Moon Sign Leo

This probably isn't the best day of the month to be considering any sort of speculation. It isn't that you are being foolish or gambling too much, it's merely that fortune doesn't favour your efforts at this time. You can improve this side of your life dramatically by the end of the week, but for now it's worth keeping your money where it is.

20 THURSDAY
Moon Age Day 22 Moon Sign Leo

For the third day in a row you would be wise to be careful and not take unnecessary chances of any sort. Stand up for yourself by all means, but it might be best to stand in the middle of any queue and not at the front, where you will attract more attention. You may decide to watch and wait until tomorrow, when the Moon moves on.

21 FRIDAY
Moon Age Day 23 Moon Sign Virgo

What a contrast to yesterday. Now you can show yourself to be very assertive, and needn't take no for an answer with regard to anything you see as being important. Neither will you be in the market for an argument, because you can stamp on anyone's opposition long before it gets to any sort of fall out.

22 SATURDAY
Moon Age Day 24 Moon Sign Virgo

You can afford to remain fairly passionate about your ideals and opinions, but not so much that you will let this get in the way of seeking a carefree and easy-going sort of weekend. All the same some of your ideas may be contentious, and you can't expect to be flavour of the month when you wear your personal badges on your sleeve.

23 SUNDAY
Moon Age Day 25 Moon Sign Libra

Trends support a more reasonable approach, in which you are less inclined to force your ideas onto others. This has been a strange departure for you because although Aquarius is a great thinker and even an intellectual, it isn't normally your way to dominate situations or people. An apology might just be called for today.

24 MONDAY
Moon Age Day 26 Moon Sign Libra

Make sure that you pay attention today, because knowing what you are talking about can make all the difference to the eventual outcome of a number of different situations. It's worth spending some of your time today thinking up ways to make your partner or lover more comfortable, and showing your charitable side.

146

25 TUESDAY
Moon Age Day 27 Moon Sign Scorpio

There isn't any doubt at present about how attractive you can make yourself to others. This could lead to the odd embarrassing situation, especially since you can be quite naïve on occasions. What you take for natural kindness and someone's warm disposition could turn out to be much more!

26 WEDNESDAY
Moon Age Day 28 Moon Sign Scorpio

It's time to stamp your personality onto certain situations, only now you can do so in a truly Aquarian way, without being bossy about it. Whilst others flap around in the shallows of life you are willing to head to deeper water, and you are about as impressive in your actions as your positive and happy-go-lucky sign can be.

27 THURSDAY
Moon Age Day 29 Moon Sign Scorpio

Your mental prowess deepens, and when it comes to thinking things through nobody could beat you today. Anything really odd could capture your interest and you may also show a great fondness for history or culture around this time. People see you as being particularly intelligent – which only goes to show how perceptive they are!

28 FRIDAY
Moon Age Day 0 Moon Sign Sagittarius

Life should be filled with possibilities at the moment, even if there are also one or two small disappointments. These are likely to come from the direction of practical efforts, some of which might have to be repeated. That shouldn't bother you much because you need to know that everything you do has been undertaken well.

29 SATURDAY
Moon Age Day 1 Moon Sign Sagittarius

Look out for those mechanical and electrical devices, all of which may seem to have a down on you today. It might be best not to interfere too much and to allow people who know better what they are doing to sort things out. Meanwhile you can think up newer and better ways to spoil your friends and to motivate your relatives.

30 SUNDAY   *Moon Age Day 2   Moon Sign Capricorn*

A twelfth-house Moon offers a chance for a quieter sort of Sunday, though one that can also be serene and comfortable. Aquarius does have a fondness for luxury on occasions, and this could be your chance to put your feet up. If you insist on being active, it's worth doing something that proves to be mentally stimulating too.

December
2008

1 MONDAY
Moon Age Day 3   Moon Sign Capricorn

It's up to you today to put in that extra bit of effort that can really make a difference. The planets say right now that if you leave things alone, that's the way they will stay, whereas if you interfere with life a little, almost anything is possible. You needn't allow anyone to push you to the back of the queue today, either at work or socially.

2 TUESDAY
Moon Age Day 4   Moon Sign Capricorn

This is likely to be a potentially good day for love, though more of the dreamy, poetical sort than the forceful, caveman type. In some respects a quieter time works best, but sandwiched between some strong planetary aspects and the arrival of the Moon into the sign of Aquarius, that isn't going to be the case for very long.

3 WEDNESDAY
Moon Age Day 5   Moon Sign Aquarius

The lunar high for December comes early in the month and offers you more energy, greater know-how and a strong intuition. Today you can stretch time to such an extent that almost anything is possible. You can be especially co-operative at the moment, so some of your successes could well be shared with colleagues or friends.

4 THURSDAY
Moon Age Day 6   Moon Sign Aquarius

If things are still going your way, you may not want to slow things down at all. Not everyone has your staying power so there could be occasions when it will be necessary to go it alone, but even this is no real problem just now. You can afford to push your luck a little, but despite the Moon's position this is not a time for overt gambling.

5 FRIDAY
Moon Age Day 7 Moon Sign Pisces

If there is one thing you relish at the moment it's a challenge. You can capitalise on any opportunity to pit your wits against people you respect as being good competitors, and you can be especially fair in your attitude right now. Keep your ears open because even a casual conversation could carry important messages.

6 SATURDAY
Moon Age Day 8 Moon Sign Pisces

Not everyone might agree with you today, particularly in a domestic sense. That's why you may have to make some compromises at home this weekend. A fair approach works best, whether the disagreement is simple, or more serious.

7 SUNDAY
Moon Age Day 9 Moon Sign Pisces

OK, so this isn't the best part of the year as far as the weather is concerned but that needn't prevent you from having a good time. Winter can be quite depressing, especially when you know there are months of it to come, but right now you can be inventive and curious. Why not think of somewhere to go that is completely different?

8 MONDAY
Moon Age Day 10 Moon Sign Aries

If you want to make things happen in a concrete sense, this is the part of the month to get moving. There can be significant developments at work for some, whilst other Aquarians could be making changes to their social lives. In many respects it's off with the old and on with the new – which is always of interest to your zodiac sign.

9 TUESDAY
Moon Age Day 11 Moon Sign Aries

What a great time this is for entertaining the crowds. Your powers of communication have seldom been better and you are extremely confident about yourself and the bearing you can have on the lives of others. When you are not out in front of a crowd you can afford to be more contemplative and to look deep inside yourself.

10 WEDNESDAY   *Moon Age Day 12 Moon Sign Taurus*

This great balance between your outward-facing self and your inward-looking qualities continues today, giving you everything you need to think and act in a positive and yet thoughtful manner. You can persuade practically everyone to like you at the moment, though of course there are bound to be exceptions.

11 THURSDAY   *Moon Age Day 13 Moon Sign Taurus*

Look out for sudden opportunities to broaden your experience base, and don't turn down invitations that seem exciting, even if some of these unnerve you a little. You are both braver and more intrepid than you sometimes think, and especially so at this stage of December. People from the past may well feature in your life again.

12 FRIDAY   *Moon Age Day 14 Moon Sign Gemini*

Being an Aquarian and so therefore always busy, it might only just have occurred to you that Christmas is just around the corner. Now is the time to get cracking, particularly if there are lots of things that need organising and maybe all those presents to buy. By all means put in some effort, though you needn't panic just yet.

13 SATURDAY   *Moon Age Day 15 Moon Sign Gemini*

This may turn out to be the best day of the month for all mental activities – everything from a simple crossword to an appearance on a television quiz show! Of course the former is more likely than the latter, but either way you will be fascinated by anything that taxes your mind and which causes you to realise just how bright you are.

14 SUNDAY   *Moon Age Day 16 Moon Sign Cancer*

Standing up for yourself should be no problem now, though you need to avoid defending yourself before you are even attacked. This may not turn out to be the best family Sunday of the month, particularly if everyone seems to have different ideas and won't listen to yours – which of course are the best of all.

15 MONDAY
Moon Age Day 17 Moon Sign Cancer

Make the most of today as far as work and practical matters are concerned, because the two-day lunar low is coming along. If there is anything that needs doing as a matter of urgency, you can't really afford to leave it any longer, and if ever the adage 'strike whilst the iron is hot' was applicable to you, it is especially true now.

16 TUESDAY
Moon Age Day 18 Moon Sign Leo

Be prepared for a few disappointments, or at the very least for a short interlude when you might doubt your own capabilities. Actually there's nothing wrong with anything you are doing, it's simply that you may not have your accustomed confidence. The time is right to seek some reassurance from friends.

17 WEDNESDAY
Moon Age Day 19 Moon Sign Leo

This is not an ideal time to gamble. Instead it's worth taking periods out from the rat race. Aquarius has a very contemplative side to its nature and you need to recognise and use that fact whilst the Moon remains in Leo. Even the lunar low can be of significant use if the period and circumstances it brings are used to your advantage.

18 THURSDAY
Moon Age Day 20 Moon Sign Virgo

It might seem as though you are a long way from reaching some of your dreams, but that's just the residue of the lunar low causing you to be a little pessimistic. As today wears on you can afford to be more and more cheerful and quite willing to join in with the fun and games that others are creating. Your own efforts come later.

19 FRIDAY
Moon Age Day 21 Moon Sign Virgo

Frustration is possible at the moment if you sense that limitations are being placed upon you, and that could cause you to react. In discussions you could be slightly prickly, but in the main you manage to understand that not everyone thinks the same. If anything really annoys you today it is likely to be people who are selfish.

20 SATURDAY
Moon Age Day 22 Moon Sign Libra

The weekend could bring a further realisation that Christmas is close. Today offers an opportunity to dash about from one shop to another, or else to find that perfect Christmas tree, only to watch it shed all its needles on the carpet. Never mind, that's what the festive season is about, and you can make sure there are plenty of laughs.

21 SUNDAY
Moon Age Day 23 Moon Sign Libra

You can continue to be light-hearted and happy to fall in line with what your friends and especially your partner want to do. There is a strong sense of curiosity about you at the moment, and you not only want to know that things happen, but why they occur, which might mean a bit of digging. Your love life should be comfortable.

22 MONDAY
Moon Age Day 24 Moon Sign Scorpio

Be prepared to do whatever you have to at work so that you can relax across the holidays without worrying about professional matters. This would be an especially good day to mix business with pleasure and to show your colleagues just how much you appreciate them. It is, however, not an ideal time to overindulge.

23 TUESDAY
Moon Age Day 25 Moon Sign Scorpio

Only two days to go, and you may still be way behind with your final preparations. Does this really worry you? Things will happen whether you monitor them or not, and everyone will manage to have a good time, even without each little detail being perfect. It's time for Aquarius to relax, you just don't realise it yet.

24 WEDNESDAY
Moon Age Day 26 Moon Sign Scorpio

Christmas Eve offers a warm glow and a sense of nostalgia regarding the way things used to be. Of course they never really were much different, it's just what the festive season does to everyone. Make the most of a deep sense of family affection and a desire to express the way you feel, especially to your lover.

25 THURSDAY   *Moon Age Day 27 Moon Sign Sagittarius*

Today could bring you much that you expected but also something that will be a real surprise – and it may not be wrapped in paper and tied with a ribbon. Make the most of any chance to get out of the house, because if you are forced to stay in with the turkey and mistletoe all day you might be chewing the carpet by the evening!

26 FRIDAY   *Moon Age Day 28 Moon Sign Sagittarius*

Once again you need change and diversity, and no matter how much family members demand your attention you would be better off seeking the company of friends at some stage today. The trouble is that even if you remain active and enterprising, you may have little or no way to utilise this side of your nature whilst the Christmas period continues.

27 SATURDAY   *Moon Age Day 0 Moon Sign Capricorn*

Looking at your depleted finances is probably not the best thing to be doing at the moment, though you can probably find something interesting to do today that costs you little or nothing. Party hats and streamers can only excite you for so long, and what you definitely need right now is something that isn't concerned with eating.

28 SUNDAY   *Moon Age Day 1 Moon Sign Capricorn*

You can afford to feel slightly more relaxed today and more willing to go with the flow than seems to have been the case across the last few days. Be prepared to respond to the demands of others. However, on the whole you stand a good chance of enjoying this particular day.

29 MONDAY   *Moon Age Day 2 Moon Sign Capricorn*

You have what it takes to end the year on a very high note, but for today at least you can be more introspective but at least somewhat less restless than of late. Your mind tends to go back in time and you are bitten once again by the Christmas nostalgia bug. Why not get in touch with friends and relatives who live a long way off?

30 TUESDAY
Moon Age Day 3 Moon Sign Aquarius

What a fine way to end a year! The Moon is back in Aquarius and you should be up for just about anything. If you put in a little preparation ahead of tomorrow's celebrations, you should enjoy them all the more. Don't allow pointless rules and regulations to get in the way, because for the moment you can make things up as you go along.

31 WEDNESDAY
Moon Age Day 4 Moon Sign Aquarius

You continue to be on fine form, and could be the one dancing in the fountains by midnight. No matter what your age you are young at heart and therefore extremely good to have around. A year-end flutter could work out well for you, and it seems as though you can't put a foot wrong. Just don't let things get too out of hand.

RISING SIGNS FOR AQUARIUS

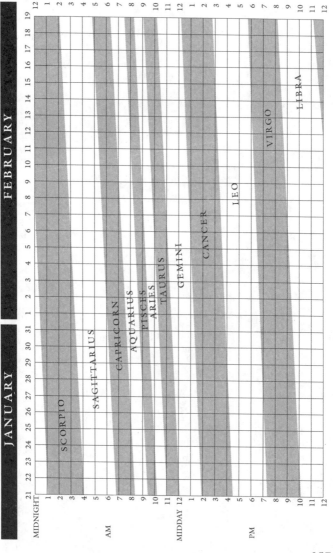

RISING SIGNS FOR VOYAGERS

THE ZODIAC, PLANETS AND CORRESPONDENCES

The Earth revolves around the Sun once every calendar year, so when viewed from Earth the Sun appears in a different part of the sky as the year progresses. In astrology, these parts of the sky are divided into the signs of the zodiac and this means that the signs are organised in a circle. The circle begins with Aries and ends with Pisces.

Taking the zodiac sign as a starting point, astrologers then work with all the positions of planets, stars and many other factors to calculate horoscopes and birth charts and tell us what the stars have in store for us.

The table below shows the planets and Elements for each of the signs of the zodiac. Each sign belongs to one of the four Elements: Fire, Air, Earth or Water. Fire signs are creative and enthusiastic; Air signs are mentally active and thoughtful; Earth signs are constructive and practical; Water signs are emotional and have strong feelings.

It also shows the metals and gemstones associated with, or corresponding with, each sign. The correspondence is made when a metal or stone possesses properties that are held in common with a particular sign of the zodiac.

Finally, the table shows the opposite of each star sign – this is the opposite sign in the astrological circle.

Placed	Sign	Symbol	Element	Planet	Metal	Stone	Opposite
1	Aries	Ram	Fire	Mars	Iron	Bloodstone	Libra
2	Taurus	Bull	Earth	Venus	Copper	Sapphire	Scorpio
3	Gemini	Twins	Air	Mercury	Mercury	Tiger's Eye	Sagittarius
4	Cancer	Crab	Water	Moon	Silver	Pearl	Capricorn
5	Leo	Lion	Fire	Sun	Gold	Ruby	Aquarius
6	Virgo	Maiden	Earth	Mercury	Mercury	Sardonyx	Pisces
7	Libra	Scales	Air	Venus	Copper	Sapphire	Aries
8	Scorpio	Scorpion	Water	Pluto	Plutonium	Jasper	Taurus
9	Sagittarius	Archer	Fire	Jupiter	Tin	Topaz	Gemini
10	Capricorn	Goat	Earth	Saturn	Lead	Black Onyx	Cancer
11	Aquarius	Waterbearer	Air	Uranus	Uranium	Amethyst	Leo
12	Pisces	Fishes	Water	Neptune	Tin	Moonstone	Virgo